Country Locator for Volume 10

BELARUS, RUSSIAN FEDERATION, AND UKRAINE

The following countries, dependencies, and states are covered in the thirteen-volume encyclopedia *World and Its Peoples: Europe*. Detailed discussion of the following can be found in the volumes indicated in parentheses.

Albania (12)
Andorra (2)
Austria (7)
Belarus (10)
Belgium (4)
Bosnia and Herzegovina (12)
Bulgaria (11)
Croatia (12)
Cyprus (11)
Czech Republic (7)
Denmark (9)
Estonia (8)
Faeroe Islands (9)

Finland (9)
France (2)
Germany (3)
Gibraltar (5)
Greece (11)
Guernsey (1)
Hungary (7)
Iceland (9)
Ireland (1)
Isle of Man (1)
Italy (6)
Jersey (1)
Kosovo (12)

Latvia (8)
Liechtenstein (7)
Lithuania (8)
Luxembourg (4)
Macedonia (12)
Malta (6)
Moldova (11)
Monaco (2)
Montenegro (12)
Netherlands (4)
Norway (9)
Poland (8)
Portugal (5)

Romania (11)
Russian Federation (10)
San Marino (6)
Serbia (12)
Slovakia (7)
Slovenia (12)
Spain (5)
Sweden (9)
Switzerland (3)
Ukraine (10)
United Kingdom (1)
Vatican City (6)

EUROPE

10

BELARUS, RUSSIAN FEDERATION, AND UKRAINE

Marshall Cavendish
Reference
New York

SET CONSULTANTS

Jeremy Black, Department of History, School of Humanities and Social Sciences, University of Exeter, England

John Harrington, Department of Geography, Kansas State University, Manhattan

Pat Morris, formerly School of Biological Sciences, Royal Holloway, University of London, England

Ceri Peach, School of Geography, University of Oxford, England

John Rennie Short, Department of Geography and Public Policy, University of Maryland, Baltimore

VOLUME CONSULTANTS

Birgit Beumers, Department of Russian, University of Bristol, England

Evgeny Dobrenko, Department of Russian and Slavonic Studies, University of Sheffield, England

Hari Rorlich, University of Southern California (Library System), Los Angeles

WRITERS

M. A. Arshinova, Faculty of Geography, M. V. Lomonosov Moscow State University, Russia

Olga Bogdanova, Peter the Great Museum of Anthropology and Ethnography (Kunstkamera) of the Russian Academy of Sciences, Saint Petersburg, Russia

Sergey I. Bolysov, Faculty of Geography, M. V. Lomonosov Moscow State University, Russia

Michelle Felton, School of Geographical Sciences, University of Bristol, England

Rinas V. Kashbrasiev, Department of Marketing and Economics, Valdosta State University, Georgia, and Kazan State University, Republic of Tatarstan, Russia

Alex Kharytanovich, Minsk, Belarus

Igor Kotin, Peter the Great Museum of Anthropology and Ethnography (Kunstkamera) of the Russian Academy of Sciences, Saint Petersburg, Russia

Svetlana Kyullenen, Saint Petersburg State University of Culture and Arts, Russia

Pavel Ovseiko, Jesus College, University of Oxford, England

Alexey P. Seregin, Department of Geobotany, Faculty of Biology, M. V. Lomonosov Moscow State University, Russia

Anna Sokolova, N. Mikluho-Maklay Institute of Ethnology and Anthropology, Russian Academy of Sciences, Moscow, Russia

Ksenia Vozdigan, Russian Christian Academy of Humanities, Saint Petersburg, Russia

For **MARSHALL CAVENDISH**
Publisher: Paul Bernabeo
Project Editor: Stephanie Driver
Production Manager: Alan Tsai
Indexer: Cynthia Crippen, AEIOU, Inc.

For **BROWN REFERENCE GROUP**
Consultant Editor: Clive Carpenter
Deputy Editors: Graham Bateman, Derek Hall, Peter Lewis, Briony Ryles
Cartography: Encompass Graphics Ltd
Picture Research: Martin Anderson, Andrew Webb
Managing Editor: Tim Harris

For **A GOOD THING, INC.**
Page Production: Howard Petlack

This publication represents the opinions and views of the authors based on personal experience, knowledge, and research. The information in this book serves as a general guide only. The authors and publisher have used their best efforts in preparing this book and disclaim liability rising directly and indirectly from the use and application of this book.

Other Marshall Cavendish Offices:
Marshall Cavendish Ltd. 5th Floor, 32-38 Saffron Hill, London EC1N 8 FH, UK • Marshall Cavendish International (Asia) Private Limited, 1 New Industrial Road, Singapore 536196 • Marshall Cavendish International (Thailand) Co Ltd. 253 Asoke, 12th Flr, Sukhumvit 21 Road, Klongtoey Nua, Wattana, Bangkok 10110, Thailand • Marshall Cavendish (Malaysia) Sdn Bhd, Times Subang, Lot 46, Subang Hi-Tech Industrial Park, Batu Tiga, 40000 Shah Alam, Selangor Darul Ehsan, Malaysia

Marshall Cavendish is a trademark of Times Publishing Limited

All websites were available and accurate when this book was sent to press.

Library of Congress Cataloging-in-Publication Data

World and its peoples. Europe.
    p. cm.
    Includes bibliographical references and index.
    ISBN 978-0-7614-7883-6 (set : alk. paper) -- ISBN 978-0-7614-7884-3 (v. 1 : alk. paper) -- ISBN 978-0-7614-7887-4 (v. 2 : alk. paper) -- ISBN 978-0-7614-7889-8 (v. 3 : alk. paper) -- ISBN 978-0-7614-7890-4 (v. 4 : alk. paper) -- ISBN 978-0-7614-7892-8 (v. 5 : alk. paper) -- ISBN 978-0-7614-7893-5 (v. 6 : alk. paper) -- ISBN 978-0-7614-7894-2 (v. 7 : alk. paper) -- ISBN 978-0-7614-7896-6 (v. 8 : alk. paper) -- ISBN 978-0-7614-7897-3 (v. 9 : alk. paper) -- ISBN 978-0-7614-7900-0 (v. 10 : alk. paper) -- ISBN 978-0-7614-7902-4 (v. 11 : alk. paper) -- ISBN 978-0-7614-7903-1 (v. 12 : alk. paper) -- ISBN 978-0-7614-7904-8 (v. 13 : alk. paper)
    1. Europe--Geography--Encyclopedias. 2. Europe--Civilization--Encyclopedias. 3. Europe--History--Encyclopedias. I. Marshall Cavendish Corporation. II. Title: Europe.
    D900.W67 2009
    940.03--dc22

                                                                    2009004321

12 11 10 09 1 2 3 4 5

Printed in Malaysia

PHOTOGRAPHIC CREDITS
Front cover: Kim Steele/Photodisc/Getty Images; Shutterstock: Pavel Losevsky bl, iNNOCENt br.
iStockphoto: Adrian Beesley 1431, Bernard Loic 1400, Ray Roper 1392; **photos.com**: 1326, 1328, 1329, 1333, 1361, 1366, 1378; **Robert Hunt Library**: 1364; **Shutterstock**: alexford 1375, Alix Alvary 1402, ansem 1317, Tim Arbaev 1345, Yury Asotov 1360, Alexey Averiyanov 1287, 1382, Suzanne Bickerdike 1368, Natalia Bratslavsky 1427, Yuriy Brykaylo 1410, 1430, Alexander Chelmodeev 1336, Vitaliy Cheusov 1409, Commit 1304, Dominator 1391, Evgeny Victorovich Dontsov 1350, 1393, Denis Dryashkin 1404, Anna Dzondzua 1349, EuToch 1385, Helen & Vlad Filatov 1325, FotoSergio 1337, Tatiana Grozetskaya 1310, iNNOCENt 1321, Alexander Kalina 1420, Sergey Kamshylin 1428, Vita Khorzhevska 1433, Georgy Ivanovich Khrushchev 1358, Fedor Konovalov 1407, Valery Kraynov 1323, Gennady Kudelya 1429, Oleg Lazarenko 1423, Natalia Lisovskaya 1398, Pavel Losevsky 1389, 1395, 1403, Lucertolone 1319, Valery Valentinovich Lukyaov 1411, Dmitry Maslov 1387, Stanislav Mikhalev 1303, Nethunter 1351, nyasha 1352, Olexa 1426, Mihail Anatolevich Orlov 1386, osov 1424, Tomasz Parys 1311, George Allan Penton 1373, Stanislav Perov 1394, Sergey Petrov 1381, Dimitry Pichugin 1309, Mikhail Pogosov 1315, 1370, posztos 1376, ppl 1332, Andrey Sarymsakov 1421, semenovp 1348, SergioZ 1306, Alexander Shingarev 1405, Natalia Shmeliova 1379, Juliya W. Shumskaya 1384, Vasily Smirnov 1372, 1383, George Spade 1313, 1413, tkachuk 1435, ukrphoto 1377, Anke van Wyk 1314, Elena Yakusheva 1340, yuri4u80 1344, Andy Z. 1418, Alexey Zarubin 1342, 1346, Serg Zastavkin 1305, 1399, Kirill Vladimirovich Zdorov 1406, Zimins@NET 1401.

CONTENTS

Geography and Climate

Belarus, the Russian Federation, and Ukraine are three Slavic nations that became independent upon the collapse of the Soviet Union. Russia is the world's largest nation by area, stretching across 11 time zones, from the Baltic Sea to the North Pacific Ocean.

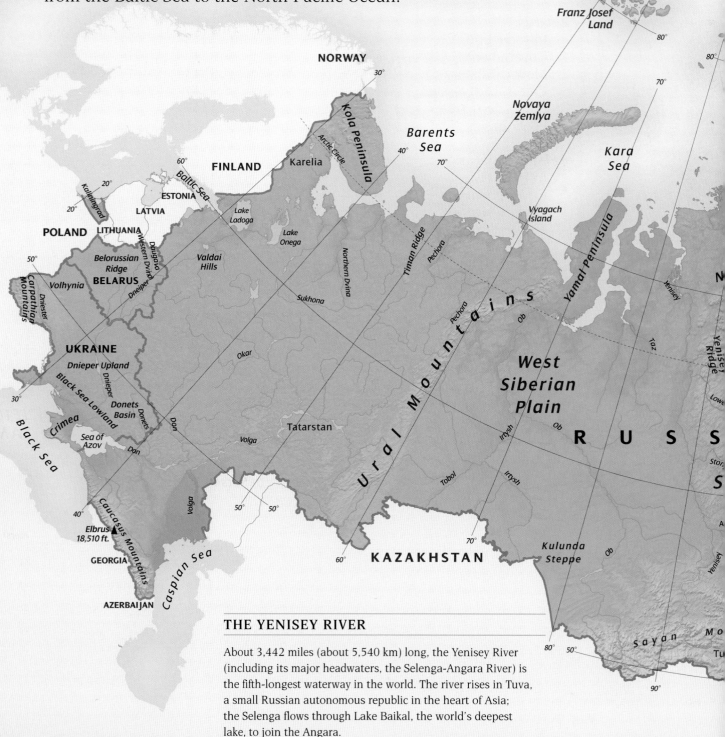

THE YENISEY RIVER

About 3,442 miles (about 5,540 km) long, the Yenisey River (including its major headwaters, the Selenga-Angara River) is the fifth-longest waterway in the world. The river rises in Tuva, a small Russian autonomous republic in the heart of Asia; the Selenga flows through Lake Baikal, the world's deepest lake, to join the Angara.

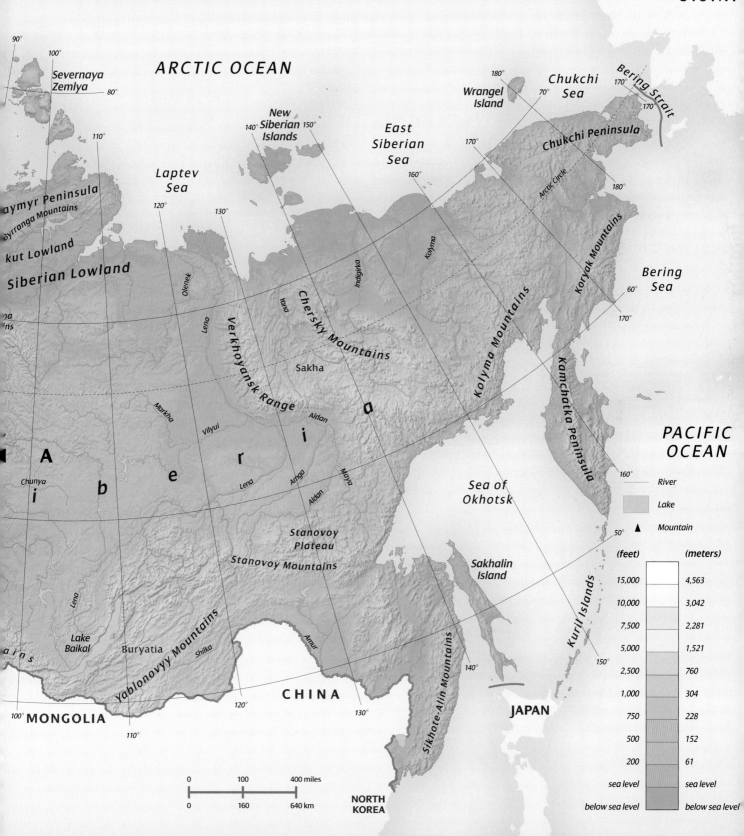

U.S.A.

ARCTIC OCEAN

90°
100°
Severnaya Zemlya 80°
110°

Byrranga Mountains
aymyr Peninsula
kut Lowland
Siberian Lowland
ns

New Siberian Islands 140° 150°
Laptev Sea 120°
130°

East Siberian Sea 160°

180° 170°
70°
Chukchi Sea
Wrangel Island
170°
Chukchi Peninsula

170° 170°

Bering Strait

Olenek
Lena
Yana
Chersky Mountains
Verkhoyansk Range
Indigirka
Kolyma
Arctic Circle
180°

Koryak Mountains

60°
Bering Sea
170°

Sakha

S i b e r i a

Chunya
A
Markha
Vilyui
Lena
i b e r
Arnga
Aldan
Lena
Aldan
Maya

Kolyma Mountains

Kamchatka Peninsula

160°

PACIFIC OCEAN

Sea of Okhotsk

50°

Stanovoy Plateau
Stanovoy Mountains

Sakhalin Island

Lena
Lake Baikal
Buryatia
Shilka
Amur

Yablonovyy Mountains

ins

120°
130°
140°
150°

Sikhote-Alin Mountains

Kuril Islands

River

Lake

▲ *Mountain*

(feet)   (meters)

15,000   4,563

10,000   3,042

7,500   2,281

5,000   1,521

2,500   760

1,000   304

750   228

500   152

200   61

sea level   sea level

below sea level   below sea level

100°
MONGOLIA
110°

CHINA

JAPAN

0   100   400 miles
0   160   640 km

NORTH KOREA

The Land of Belarus, Russia, and Ukraine

The Russian Federation, Belarus, and Ukraine cover one-sixth of the world's land area. This huge area contains a great variety of natural zones and physical and climatic conditions, from uninhabited Arctic islands and high-mountain glaciers to Mediterranean scrub forests of the Black Sea coast and semidesert adjoining the Caspian Sea. Nearly half of the region is permanently frozen.

The physical division of Belarus, Russia, and Ukraine into major regions is complicated. There are hundreds of distinct physical regions within the vast area formed by these three countries. However, a relatively small number of broad regions, which contain within them considerable variety, may be recognized.

Belarus is largely a plain, occupying the northwestern part of the East European Plain, a continuation of the North European Plain. The major part of Ukraine also lies within this plain, although the westernmost and southernmost parts of the country are mountainous. The terrain within Russia is more diverse. Vast plains are divided east-west into climatic-vegetation zones—tundra, taiga, mixed forest, steppe—from north to south, and these huge ecosystems occupy most of European Russia and the greater part of Siberia. Mountainous regions are largely peripheral, around the southern and eastern edges of the extensive plains. Southern Siberia and the Russian Far East are the most mountainous regions, with extremely diverse climatic conditions and habitats.

The major broad geographical regions into which Russia, along with Belarus and Ukraine, can be divided are: the East European or Russian Plain, the Baltic Shield, the Carpathian Mountains, Crimea, and the Caucasus (all in Europe); the Urals, which form the border between Europe and Asia; the Western Siberian Lowland, Eastern Siberia, the Altay and Sayan mountains, the Baikal region, and the Siberian northeast (all in Siberia); and Beringia, the Kamchatka-Kuril volcanic region, the Amur region, and Sakhalin (all in the Russian Far East).

EUROPEAN RUSSIA

European Russia accounts for 40 percent of the area of Europe, although the Asiatic part of Russia accounts for the greater part of the nation's area. The majority of Russians—more than 75 percent—live in European Russia, which may be divided into five or six main geographical regions. By convention, European Russia is said to end at the Ural Mountains in the east, but the southern border is debated. Some geographers opt for the crest of the Caucasus Mountains, placing Georgia, Armenia, and Azerbaijan (to the south) physically in Asia. However, modern practice is to regard Georgia and Armenia, and sometimes Azerbaijan as well, as European nations. Other geographers place the physical boundary between Europe and Asia in the south along the line of the Manych River, extending the line to the estuary of the Don River; this places the Caucasian region of Russia in Asia.

THE EAST EUROPEAN PLAIN

The East European, or Russian, Plain covers an area of more than 1,500,000 square miles (about 4,000,000 sq. km), stretching some 1,000 miles (about 1,600 km) from east to west and around 1,500 miles (about 2,400 km) from north to south. Its vast, relatively flat surface averages about 560 feet (about 170 m) above sea level with the highest point in the Valdai Hills, near Moscow, reaching only 1,125 feet (343 m).

The plain, which extends from the Baltic Sea in the west through all of Belarus, most of Ukraine, and the greater part of European Russia, comprises a number of separate lowlands and low hills and ends in the east at the Ural Mountains. In the north, the plain reaches the Arctic Ocean, while in the south it reaches the Caspian Sea and the Caucasus foothills. The region rises in its central part, Middle Russia, to form a watershed for

RIVERS OF BELARUS, RUSSIA, AND UKRAINE

River	Length in miles	Length in km
Yenisey-Angara-Selenga	3,442	5,540
Ob-Irtysh*	3,361	5,409
Lena-Kirenga	2,734	4,400
Amur-Argun*	2,700	4,345
Volga	2,193	3,530
Lower Tunguska	1,857	2,989
Vilyui	1,647	2,650
Kolyma	1,615	2,600
Ural	1,578	2,540
Dneiper	1,420	2,285
Olenek	1,411	2,270
Don	1,224	1,969

* Not all the course of these waterways flows through the region.

Lake Baikal, in southern Siberia, is the deepest freshwater lake in the world.

headwaters of major waterways, which flow to the Arctic Ocean, the Baltic Sea, and the interior Caspian Sea. In the southeast, the Caspian Depression, which is below sea level, has a flat surface.

Glaciation, ending some 10,000 years ago, deposited thick moraine, a combination of loam and granitic boulders, across much of the plain. From north to south, the East European Plain comprises a series of broad east-west belts. In the far north is a frozen Arctic waste, which is hardly populated. South of the frozen zone is tundra, a sparsely peopled woodless region. South again are forest-tundra, taiga (coniferous forest), and mixed forest zones, which together contain Europe's greatest reserves of timber. Forest-steppe and steppe lie to the south in a region that has a rich soil (black earth or chernozem), which supports extensive agriculture, based on cereals. In places, the zone is poorly drained and marshy, and in Belarus, the Pripyat Marshes lie to the south of the low Belorussian Ridge that runs southwest to northeast across Belarus. The steppes give way in the southeast to semidesert and desert near the Caspian Sea.

The region contains many of Russia's major cities—including Moscow, the national capital of Russia, with a population in the metropolitan area of 12,400,000 in 2006, and Saint Petersburg, Russia's main port, with a population of 4,581,000 in the same year—and the greater part of Russia's industries. Many cities lie along the major waterways of the region, particularly the Volga

(Nizhny Novgorod, Kazan, Samara, and Volgograd), Dneiper (Kiev, the Ukrainian national capital, and Dnipropetrovs'k), and Don (Rostov-na-Donu) rivers. These and other major waterways have been extensively dammed to provide hydroelectric power, and their courses are lined by large reservoirs. Other major centers of population have grown around natural resources, for example, the industrial Donets Basin (or Donbas) coalfield in eastern Ukraine and extending into Russia.

The exclave of Kaliningrad, lying between Poland and Lithuania along the Baltic coast, may be regarded as part of the plain. Before 1945, Kaliningrad was called Königsberg and was part of Germany. This small region is now home to peoples who were brought from other parts of the former Soviet Union after the region's German population was expelled.

THE BALTIC SHIELD

The Baltic Shield is a large area of old hard rocks, underlying most of Scandinavia and extending into the far northwest of Russia. This small region comprises Karelia in the south and the Kola Peninsula in the north, and ends in the south at two large lakes, Ladoga (the largest lake in Europe) and Onega. Forested Karelia is lightly populated. The Kola Peninsula is a plateau in the east but is formed of mountainous massifs in the west, rising to 3,907 feet (1,191 m). The region includes Arctic and tundra coastal lowlands along the White Sea and is rich in minerals.

The Black Sea coast at Yalta in Crimea, Ukraine.

THE CARPATHIANS

The Carpathian Mountains are a ridge of fold mountains in western Ukraine. The uplands form three distinct chains, rising to 6,762 feet (2,061 m) at Hoverla, the highest point in Ukraine, although the average heights of the peaks are about 3,300 feet (about 1,000 m) above sea level in the northwest and more than 4,900 feet (about 1,500 m) in the southeast. The region is agricultural in the valleys and forested along the ridges, and it is divided by major waterways, including the Tisza and Uzh rivers.

CRIMEA

Different from most of the rest of Ukraine to the north of it, the Crimean Peninsula has a Mediterranean-type climate. The Crimean Mountains is the general name for three almost parallel ridges, which run along the southern coast of the peninsula. They increase in height from north to south, with the highest peak, Mount Roman-Kosh, which rises to 5,062 feet (1,543 m), near the coast. The main southern ridge, which protects a string of coastal resorts, is wooded, with meadows on the upper reaches of the plateau. Like the Donbas industrial region in eastern Ukraine, Crimea is also mainly Russian speaking.

THE CAUCASUS MOUNTAINS

The Caucasus Mountains are geologically young, and some of their peaks are the remains of extinct volcanoes. Earthquakes are relatively common in the region. The Greater Caucasus Range is the highest part of Russia, with Elbrus, along the border with Georgia, reaching 18,510 feet (5,642 m). Elbrus, an extinct volcano, is usually said to be the highest mountain in Europe.

The watershed line of the Greater Caucasus Range forms the national border of the Russian Federation, and along the border lie several autonomous republics of the federation, each home to a different ethnic group. In modern times, this region has experienced considerable tension as some peoples, such as the Muslim Chechens, seek to secede. The region along the coast, from Novorossiysk to Sochi, is the only part of Russia with Mediterranean ecosystems, and diversity is great throughout the Caucasus. Tea and grapes are grown in south-facing lowlands, while large glaciers and permanent snow cover the highest peaks.

THE URALS

The Urals belong both to Europe and Asia. The uplands, which extend north into the Arctic islands of Novaya Zemlya, are the only major mountain chain in Russia to run from north to south. Stretching for 1,850 miles (about 3,000 km), the mountains cross all the habitats, from Arctic wastes to dry steppes, that characterize the East European Plain to the east. The Urals are not particularly high, with Mount Narodnaya, the highest point, reaching 6,217 feet (1,895 m). They form several broken ridges, divided by easily passable gaps; as a result, they are not a significant barrier to communication.

Geographers generally divide the Urals into several parts: southern, middle, northern, prepolar, and polar Urals, and the Pay-Khoy Ridge. The southern Urals are forested and contain three large state preserves and a national park. The low Middle Urals contain a great diversity of minerals, upon which industries are based. This area serves as the traditional gateway to Siberia from European Russia and contains the principal cities of the Urals, including Yekaterinburg (which lies east of the mountains). The northern Urals are the longest continuous highlands in the chain, while the prepolar Urals form the highest part. The polar Urals are lower and grade into the Pay-Khoy Ridge, the northernmost continental part of the Urals. A narrow strait separates low Vaigach Island from the continent, while, farther north, mountainous Novaya Zemlya consists of two islands: Yuzhny Island and Severny Island. The latter contains the largest glacier in Russia.

SIBERIA

East of the Ural foothills, Siberia is a vast natural wildness, which experiences a severe climate. Several plains form the northern part of Siberia, while southern Siberia is a mountainous region, a complicated network of plateaus, ridges, and intermontane basins. Siberia contains great natural resources, including the mineral wealth upon which the economy of modern Russia depends, but most of the resources exploited are in the more accessible, populated south, along or near the line of the Trans-Siberian Railroad. The north is almost completely covered with permafrost (ground that is permanently frozen, often to a great depth) and has few people; many of its resources are still largely untouched.

THE WESTERN SIBERIAN LOWLAND

Western Siberia is a flat, swampy lowland, which stretches from the Urals in the west to the Yenisey River in the east and from the Arctic Ocean in the north to the steppes of neighboring Kazakhstan in the south. It covers an area of about 1,100,000 square miles (about 3,000,000 sq. km), which is just under one-third the area of the United States. Low altitude, the region's flatness, and superfluous water led to the formation of huge peat bogs, which are still increasing in extent and thickness.

The region was once home to nomads, who hunted, fished, and raised reindeer, but, in the 1960s, oil was discovered in the taiga zone and natural gas was found in the tundra belt. As a result, the region is one of the most prosperous in Russia with new cities close to numerous wells that exploit western Siberia's natural resources. However, the largest cities are in the south, on drier land and closer to the main east-west route across southern Siberia. Western Siberian oil and gas now form the largest export of the Russian economy.

Tundra extends over much of Siberia.

EASTERN SIBERIA

Eastern Siberia comprises a number of uplands, plateaus, and low mountains, lying between the Yenisey and the Lena rivers, with the greater part formed by the Central Siberian Plateau. Severnaya Zemlya archipelago, in the Arctic Ocean, is a detached part of the eastern Siberian plateaus, while the Taymyr Peninsula is the northernmost part of continental Asia. The Byrranga Mountains cross the peninsula from southwest to northeast, rising to 3,760 feet (1,146 m) in the east. The North Siberian Lowland separates the Taymyr Peninsula from the Central Siberian Plateau, an extensive upland that reaches its greatest height (5,581 feet, or 1,701 m) in the north, where the Putorana Mountains are situated. The western edge of the plateau is lined by long lakes, and one of the world's richest nickel deposits is situated nearby at Norilsk, a city inside the Arctic Circle.

On the eastern side of the Central Siberian Plateau is the wide Yakut Lowland, while the Lena-Angara Plateau occupies the southern part of eastern Siberia. The Angara River, which crosses the plateau, is the only waterway flowing from Lake Baikal; it is dammed in five places to supply hydroelectric power.

The summit of Elbrus at 18,510 feet (5,642 m) is the highest mountain in Europe.

THE ALTAY AND SAYAN MOUNTAINS

The Altay-Sayanian region separates the cold Siberian taiga from the hot deserts of Central Asia. The headwaters of the Ob and the Yenisey rivers flow through the region. The Altay is the highest mountainous region of southern Siberia, with ridges in the central and eastern parts rising to 10,000–13,000 feet (about 3,000–4,000 m) above sea level. Mount Belukha, in the Altay Shan range, is the highest peak in Siberia at 14,783 feet (4,506 m). There are more than 1,000 glaciers in the Altay Mountains, covering a total area of about 230 square miles (about 600 sq. km).

The Sayan Mountains are a complicated system cut by a dense network of deep river valleys. The average height of the Sayan ridges is about 3,300–6,600 feet (about 1,000–2,000 m) above sea level, although in some places crests reach 10,000 feet (3,000 m), and Mount Munku-Sardyk rises to 11,457 feet (3,492 m). These sparsely populated regions are home to herders, and most peoples in the area are Mongoloid or other Asians rather than ethnic Russians.

THE BAIKAL REGION

Lake Baikal is the deepest lake in the world, with a depth of 5,315 feet (1,620 m). It also contains more freshwater than any other lake in the world. Many rivers supply Baikal with water, but only

the Angara drains it. This region is commonly divided into Prebaikalia and Transbaikalia. Prebaikalia includes Lake Baikal and surrounding mountain ranges: the Khamar-Daban in the south, Primorsky and Baikalsky in the west, and Barguzin in the east. Transbaikalia is a large mountainous area, crossed, in the south, by a series of wide tablelike ridges that run from southwest to northeast. They average about 3,300–5,900 feet (about 1,000–1,800 m) above sea level. Southeastern Transbaikalia, known as Dahuria, is a hilly steppe region. Northern Transbaikalia is a region of uplands and ridges, from 3,300 to 8,200 feet (about 1,000–2,500 m) high. They include the Stanovoy Mountains, and the Severo-Baikalskoye, Patomskoye, Olekmo-Charskoye, and Aldanskoye plateaus. Mount Kodar is the highest peak of the Baikal region at 9,839 feet (2,999 m). Except in the vicinity of the city of Irkutsk, west of Lake Baikal, and Ulan Ude, to the east of the lake, the Baikal region is sparsely populated.

THE SIBERIAN NORTHEAST

Lowlands occupy the coastal area of the Siberian northeast, including the Yana-Indigirka Lowland and the Kolyma Lowland on the mainland and the New Siberian Islands in the Arctic Ocean. However, the greater part of the Siberian northeast is upland, a complicated tangle of numerous ridges and plateaus. The most prominent ranges are the Verkhoyanski, Suntar-Khayata, Momski, and Chersky mountains. The Chersky Mountains include Mount Pobeda (10,325 feet, or 3,147 m). The region has a particularly severe climate, and the Verkhoyansk region has recorded some of the world's lowest temperatures, including -90°F (-68°C) in January 1885.

THE RUSSIAN FAR EAST

The Russian Far East is a diverse area along the Pacific coast. It includes lowlands and high mountains, active volcanoes, various islands, extensive regions of permafrost, and geysers. Four main subdivisions are generally recognized: Beringia, the Kamchatka-Kuril volcanic region, the Amur region, and the island of Sakhalin.

BERINGIA

Beringia, or the Northern Pacific Region, is surrounded by the cold-water masses of the East Siberian, Chukchi, and Bering seas, and the Sea of Okhotsk. Wrangel Island separates the East Siberian Sea from the Chukchi Sea; the whole island is a state preserve for tundra habitats. Beringia consists of three mountainous areas and an intermontane lowland. The mountains of the Chukchi Upland (rising to 6,047 feet, or 1,843 m) form the continental north of Beringia, while the Chukchi Peninsula is the most distant part of the Russian mainland from Moscow. Ratmanov Island, in the Bering Strait, is the easternmost point of Russia, while the Bering Strait connects the

Arctic Ocean with the Pacific Ocean and separates Eurasia and North America. The Anadyr-Penzhina Lowland is a narrow strip between the Sea of Okhotsk and the Bering Sea. The Koryak Upland stretches along the Bering Sea, reaching 8,406 feet (2,562 m) at Mount Ledyanaya. Several coastal mountain ranges, including the Kolyma Mountains in the east, line the high northern coast of the Sea of Okhotsk.

KAMCHATKA AND THE KURIL ISLANDS

The Kamchatka-Kuril volcanic region is part of the Pacific Ring of Fire, a volcanic zone that encircles the basin of the Pacific Ocean. There are 30 active and more extinct volcanoes in Kamchatka, which stretches about 750 miles (about 1,200 km) from north to south, although the maximum width of the peninsula is 300 miles (about 480 km). A mountain range forming the crest of the peninsula is separated from an eastern range by the Kamchatka River. The eastern range has a number of high volcanoes, including Klyuchevskaya Sopka, the most active volcano in the region and the highest peak of Asiatic Russia at 15,584 feet (4,750 m) above sea level.

The Kuril Islands form an arc about 750 miles (about 1,200 km) long, which extends from the southernmost cape of Kamchatka to the Japanese island of Hokkaido. The Kurils— which include seven large islands and a great number of small islands, islets, and rocks—are volcanic. The southernmost Kuril Islands were part of Japan before the end of World War II (1939–1945) and are still claimed by that country.

THE AMUR REGION

The Amur region occupies the southern part of the Russian Far East. Several plains and mountain chains occupy the region, including the Upper Zeya ridges, the Bureya Upland, and the Sikhote-Alin Mountains. The main plains of the region are the Amur-Zeya Plateau and the Middle Amur Lowland. The territory to the south and east of the Amur River is called Primorye ("land near the sea"). Primorye has a low western region and a mountainous eastern region, which includes the wide Sikhote-Alin Mountains, stretching from southwest to northeast. The Ussuri Lowland and the Khanka Lowland form a narrow western strip of Primorye, along the Chinese border. The principal city of the Amur region is the port of Vladivostok.

SAKHALIN

Sakhalin, Russia's largest island, has an area of about 29,500 square miles (about 76,400 sq. km). It is 589 miles (948 km) long, but its width does not exceed 93 miles (150 km). Two low parallel mountain ranges run through Sakhalin from north to south. Before 1945, the southern half of the island was part of Japan.

A. P. SEREGIN

Geology of Belarus, Russia, and Ukraine

Russia is divided between Europe and Asia along the line of the Ural Mountains, which separates two vast regions of remarkably stable geology.

Much of the region of Russia, Belarus, and Ukraine is formed by cratons—stable, central parts of a continental plate (one of the divisions of the lithosphere, Earth's outer layer). Cratons are typically formed from deep, thick layers of sedimentary rock (rock that is deposited in layers). Around the edges of the cratons are fold mountains, some of recent geologic formation during the last 65 million years, and others that are much older and have been eroded.

THE EAST EUROPEAN CRATON

While parts of southern Ukraine and the Caucasus are on the small Scythian Plate, most of European Russia, Belarus, and Ukraine are part of the East European Craton (part of the large Eurasian Plate). This wide, geologically stable region is formed of deep layers of sedimentary rock, which date back to Ediacaran times (600 through 545 million years ago) and earlier. The craton ends in the east at the Urals, a range of mountains that runs north-south through Russia. The Urals were formed by the collision of the East European Craton with the cratons of Siberia, to the east, some 250 million years ago, during the Permian period (290 through 248 million years ago). Earth's plates move over the semimolten layer beneath. Previously, there was an ocean between the East European Craton and those to the east, but plate movement resulted in ocean closure. The ocean floor between them, covered by thick layers of sediments, buckled and was lifted. The Urals have since been heavily eroded and are not a significant barrier in many places.

THE SIBERIAN CRATONS

The cratons that make up Siberia have a long history, having been formed in pre-Cambrian times (roughly 3 billion to 600 million years ago). The largest is the Angaran Craton or East Siberian Platform, which extends over a huge area. West of the Angaran Craton is the West Siberian Plate, which, like the Angaran Craton, contains gneiss, a coarse-grained metamorphic rock (a rock that has been changed by heat, pressure, or chemical action); marble; quartzite; and conglomerates, rocks formed from fragments. The flat West Siberian Plate is the second-largest lowland in the world, covering an area of nearly 3 million square miles (about 7.8 million sq. km).

The cratons were later extended around their southwestern and southeastern margins by orogenesis (mountain building). Erosion from the Angaran Craton deposited large amounts of sediments in the sea to the south. The movement of plates squeezed these deposits, and as subduction occurred—the edge of one plate passing under another—mountains known as the Altaids were formed, beginning around 850 million years ago and lasting into the Triassic period (248 to 206 million years ago).

In the meantime, the center of the East Siberian Craton was subject to the most violent event in its geological history: the formation of the Siberian Traps, the largest volcanic event of the last 500 million years. This massive igneous event occurred in the late Permian and early Triassic periods, when magma under great pressure erupted onto the surface through numerous vents. The eruption covered an area of some 770,000 square miles (around 2 million sq. km) with lava, which cooled to form the rock basalt. In the conduits through which magma flowed near the surface, deposits of copper and nickel formed.

PERIPHERAL OROGENY

The rest of the formation of the vast landmass of Russia, Belarus, and Ukraine can most simply be described as the story of orogenesis around the cratons' southern and eastern margins. The mountain chains were created in different orogenies; for example, the Carpathian Mountains in Ukraine were formed when the Tethys Sea, the sea that lay between Laurasia (the supercontinent that comprised North America, Europe, and Asia) and Gondwana (the supercontinent that was the ancestor of Africa and South America) closed. This closure started at the beginning of the Mesozoic era (248 to 65 million years ago).

The Tethys Sea extended south of the Siberian craton and closed there between 210 and 180 million years ago (during the Jurassic period, which lasted from 206 to 142 million years ago). As it did so, the sea trough, which was filled with sediments, was compressed; one continent subducted under the other; and a mountain range was added along the southern edge of the Altaids, the Cimmerides. The main ridge of the Crimean Mountains (in southern Ukraine) is a representative of this orogeny. This and the earlier Altaids were later uplifted again, from some 65 million years ago during the Alpine-Himalayan orogeny, and are now represented by the east-west ranges of southern Siberian Russia.

The largest period of mountain building, the Alpine-Himalayan orogeny, began around 65 million years ago, when the African plate moved northward toward the Eurasian plate. This process slowly closed the Tethys Sea. Rocks on the floor of the sea were severely deformed and, under pressure, they were forced to rise to form mountain chains. Sedimentary rocks in the Tethys Basin were metamorphosed. The orogeny was complex because the compression was accompanied by thrust faulting, in which large areas of uplifted rock broke away and then slid over the plate edge. This orogeny created the Caucasus Mountains along the southern border of Russia and, under pressure, uplifted other older mountain chains to the north of the main Himalayan range in Asia. The Caucasus was the scene of volcanic activity in the later stages of the orogeny. There are now no active volcanoes, but many of the rocks of the region are igneous (formed from magma or lava), including basalt and andesite. The region is, however, subject to earthquakes along fault lines within the zone of subduction.

Mountain building continues in the circum-Pacific belt, which is also known as the Pacific Ring of Fire. This extended chain of mountains includes the Kamchatka Peninsula, where the Pacific Plate is being subducted beneath the edge of the Eurasian Plate. Kamchatka is one of the most active volcanic regions in the world, with around 30 active and many more dormant volcanoes. Around 40 percent of the peninsula is covered with volcanic deposits. The peninsula also has many hot springs, geysers, and fumaroles (vents in or near volcanoes from which gases are emitted), providing additional evidence that volcanic activity is continuing. Offshore, the Kuril-Kamchatka Trench is the zone where the Pacific Plate edge is being subducted. Fault lines along the trench allow magma to well up from below, causing volcanic activity. In this region, the processes that formed the mountain chains of Russia in the past are still active, and the region is also prone to seismic activity along the faults in the trench. There are also extinct volcanic domes in northeast Russia, in the Kolyma and Indigrika river basins.

An active volcano in the Kamchatka peninsula, Russia.

GLACIATION

Large areas of Russia and Belarus were covered by thick ice sheets in the recent geological past. The last ice sheets advanced around 650,000 years ago, finally retreating 10,000 years ago, after several periods when the ice had advanced and retreated; there were, at least, four of these glacial cycles. Ice spread southward from the Arctic and northward from the high mountains of the Alpine-Himalayan system, removing soil cover and depositing it elsewhere as fertile loess.

North of the loess zone is the Black Earth Zone, where black earth (or chernozem) is the predominant soil. This soil is of much more recent formation. The region has sufficient precipitation to decay the grass litter but not sufficient to wash the resulting humus (decayed plant matter) down beyond roots in a process known as leaching. As a result, the chernozem forms a layer of fertile soil, up to 40 inches (102 cm) deep, across northern Ukraine and southern Russia, stretching into western Siberia.

The lowland marshes of Belarus are formed from glacial material (moraine) deposited at the ice front. Elsewhere in northern Russia, there are eskers, ridges formed under the ice by subglacial streams depositing moraine. However, the highlands have other glacial features, those of erosion rather than deposition. Glaciers carved U-shaped valleys, with hanging valleys (tributary valleys eroded by smaller glaciers entering the main valley at a higher level). Above the ice, jagged frost-shattered peaks formed, while cirques (basinlike depressions high on the mountainsides, where glaciers began) were also carved.

The geology of recent times is represented by deposition of clays, laying down material eroded by great waterways, and, particularly, the formation of widespread bog deposits (peat) across broad regions. For example, expanses of alluvial (water-carried) sands and loams are characteristic of river valleys in the Ob River basin, while the peat Pripyat Marshes cover much of south Belarus.

S. I. BOLYSOV, M. A. ARSHINOVA

Climate of Belarus, Russia, and Ukraine

The region formed by Russia, Belarus, and Ukraine has a great range of climates from arctic tundra conditions in the extreme north and Siberia, to arid desert conditions in the central south, and Mediterranean and humid subtropical climates in the southwest.

Russia, the largest country in the world in area, covers a huge extent in longitude and latitude, spanning some 4,100 miles (about 6,600 km) from east to west. Within this area, a great variety of terrains plays a major role in determining climatic differences and, as a result, hundreds of climatic regions may be recognized. Belarus and Ukraine are much smaller, although Ukraine is the largest country entirely within the continent of Europe and displays considerable regional variation in climate. Despite this multiplicity of climatic regions, at its simplest, some four large climatic-geographical zones can be defined. These vast regions are: northern European Russia with Belarus and northern and central Ukraine; southern Russia and southern Ukraine; Siberia; and the high mountain regions.

Most of the large area of the Russian landmass is a long distance away from the influence of the oceans. Consequently, the climate of Russia is mostly continental with strong contrasts between (warm) summer and (very cold) winter seasons and also between day and night temperatures.

Average temperatures are coldest in the most northerly areas, at the highest elevations, and farthest from the coast. There is sea ice along the northern coasts during winter, and icebreakers may be used to keep open some shipping routes along the Arctic Ocean coast and even in the Baltic Sea. The mildest temperatures are found along the Black Sea coastal area in far southwestern Russia and in southern Ukraine. Total annual precipitation is lightest in the northern areas. Rainfall is heaviest over mountain ranges that are not in the continental interior and in eastern coastal areas, particularly those districts adjoining the Sea of Okhotsk. Precipitation peaks in the early summer months in most areas of Russia, Belarus, and Ukraine.

The main influences on the climate of this vast region are the prevailing cold winds from Siberia and the Arctic; the high mountain ranges; and the distance to the surrounding oceans, the Arctic Ocean in the north and the Pacific Ocean to the east. The altitude of the land strongly influences local climate, with average temperatures being significantly lower at higher altitudes.

In Primorsky Krai in the far southeast of Russia, the warm Sea of Japan creates a moderate maritime climate.

THE NORTHERN EUROPEAN ZONE

Belarus, northern and most of central Ukraine, and the Russian Federation west of the Ural mountain range make up the large Northern European climatic zone, which is mostly low-lying with rolling hills up to around 1,000 feet (about 300 m) in elevation. This area has a generally continental climate and is influenced by winds and storms moving eastward from the Atlantic Ocean. Air masses from the west cause variable, unsettled weather, as well as frequent cloud cover. Average winter temperatures vary over this region, which is much colder in northern and eastern areas.

Moscow, the national capital of the Russian Federation, is located in the center of this zone at an elevation of 623 feet (190 m) and has a typical climate with annual precipitation of 23.6 inches (60 cm), falling throughout the year with a peak during the summer. Average maximum January temperatures are around 16°F (-9°C), with daily minimum temperatures of 3°F (-16°C). In July, daily high temperatures average 71°F (23°C), with average low temperatures of 55°F (13°C). Farther north, the winter is much colder, for example in Arkhangel'sk at latitude 65°N, where the average winter maximum temperatures are 12°F (-11°C) in January, and average low temperatures are just 1°F (-17°C).

Moscow experiences much snow during the long Russian winter.

THE SOUTHERN EUROPEAN AREA

The southern European area includes southern Ukraine and European Russia as far east as the Ural Mountains. This extensive region has a generally less extreme climate, with longer summers, although winds from Siberia can still bring extremely cold weather. The average temperatures are higher in the east and south.

The southeast is very dry and is dominated by steppe vegetation. Characteristic winds include the *sukhovey*, a strong, hot, dry wind in summer, and, in winter, the *buran*, an extremely cold, strong wind that can cause blizzards. Astrakhan, near the Caspian Sea, has an annual precipitation of just 7.8 inches (20 cm).

In the southwest, Ukraine and the Russian Federation have coastlines along the Black Sea and the Caspian Sea. This area has the mildest climate in the region, with warmer summer temperatures and less extreme cold temperatures in winter than the rest of the Russian Federation. It also has more sunshine hours per day, with up to 10 hours per day.

Simferopol, in southern Crimea along the eastern Black Sea coast, has a climate typical of this region. Average annual precipitation is 20.9 inches (53.1 cm), which falls throughout the year with a peak in mid-summer. In winter, average January daily maximum temperatures are 37°F (3°C) with average minimum temperatures being 27°F (-3°C). In the summer, average July maximum temperatures are 79°F (26°C), with average minimum temperatures of 61°F (16°C). From December through March, average temperatures remain below freezing for more than 50 percent of the days.

SIBERIA

The Siberian zone spans eastward from the Ural mountain range in central Russia to the Pacific Ocean. In the south, it stretches from the borders of China, Kazakhstan, and Mongolia, while to the north the region reaches the Arctic Ocean. This huge region includes a great variety of terrain, although Siberia consists mostly of lowlands, low plateaus, and extensive river basins. There are also rolling hills and many ridges of mountains, particularly in the northeast. The vegetation is mostly tundra type (woodless with low herbs) in the north, with taiga coniferous forest in the south.

Winters are long and severe, with frequent snowfall and extremely cold temperatures in the north. There are extensive areas of permafrost (permanently frozen ground) in the northern and eastern areas. Verkhoyansk, in the north, is one of the coldest places, with average maximum temperatures in January of -54°F (-48°C). Tomsk is typical of central Siberia, with average January maximum temperatures of 0°F (-18°C) and minimum January temperatures of -11°F (-24°C). The annual precipitation in Tomsk is around 20 inches (50.7 cm), falling mostly during the summers, which are short but relatively warm with average maximum temperatures of 73°F (23°C) in July.

Eastern Siberia along the coastline of the Pacific Ocean is strongly affected by the summer Asian monsoon, which brings moist winds from the east across the Pacific Ocean. This gives significantly heavier rainfall in summer. In winter, temperatures are very cold, and the humidity is low because the dominant wind is from the west, blowing from cold, dry, inland Siberia.

MOUNTAIN RANGES

The high mountain ranges of Russia include the Ural Mountains in the west (which separate Europe from Asia); the Chersky, Verkhiyanski, and Kolyma mountains in eastern Siberia; and the Sayan Mountains, the Altay range, and the Caucasus Mountains in the south. These high peaks are important influences on the climate of the region, as they act as obstacles to winds moving over the continent.

The high mountains also tend to capture moisture from warm moist winds that travel over the peaks because warm moist air cools as it rises. As a result, the air can hold less water, and moisture precipitates out as rain or snow. Consequently, land on the leeward side of the mountain range, the side away from prevailing moist air masses, may be in a rain shadow. Rain shadows are areas with a much drier climate, because the winds have lost most of their moisture after having passed over the mountains.

Ulan-Ude, at an elevation of 1,690 feet (515 m) in the Sayan mountain range, near the border with Mongolia, has a typical climate with an average high temperature in January of around 0°F (-18°C) and average low temperatures of -22°F (-30°C). Average annual precipitation is relatively low at 9.9 inches (21.5 cm).

CLIMATIC HAZARDS

The extreme cold winter temperatures in most of Russia, Belarus, and Ukraine can be a health hazard, with increased risk of hypothermia and frostbite, particularly in very cold winds. Extreme cold temperatures can also damage infrastructure, particularly water pipes, which may crack and cause flooding.

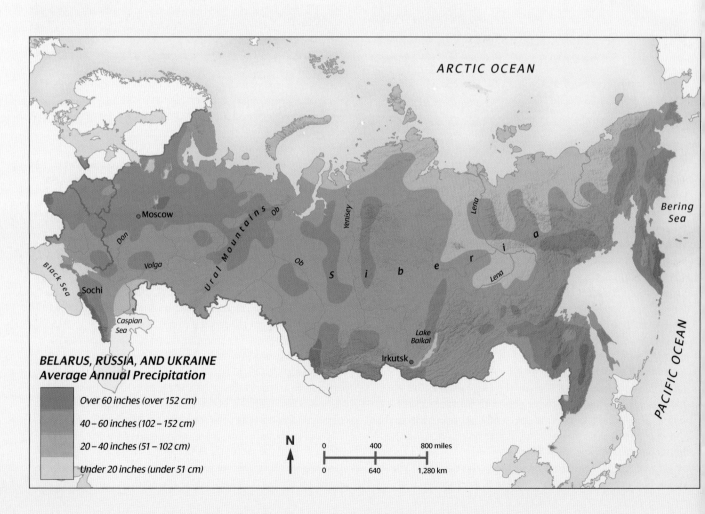

BELARUS, RUSSIA, AND UKRAINE
Average Annual Precipitation

Over 60 inches (over 152 cm)

40 – 60 inches (102 – 152 cm)

20 – 40 inches (51 – 102 cm)

Under 20 inches (under 51 cm)

N

0   400   800 miles
0   640   1,280 km

The taiga (conifer forest) landscape of Siberia marks the southernmost band of the cold Siberian climate zone.

Strong winds in winter can cause snow drifts, which affect transportation. Frozen rivers and sea ice in coastal areas makes transportation over water more hazardous in winter.

Sudden or unexpected thawing of permafrost may also present a hazard to infrastructure, as building foundations may have been built to depend on permanently frozen ground. Thawing of permafrost may cause serious damage to roads, buildings, and pipelines, and significant changes to the local vegetation. Drought occurs in some of the drier parts in the south, where agriculture is particularly vulnerable to water shortages.

CLIMATE CHANGE

Global climate change is resulting in warmer average temperatures all over Europe, and this northern region is expected to have some of the highest increases in average temperature—greater than 6.5°F to 8°F (3.5°C to 4.5°C) from 1990 through 2080. The largest changes in temperature will be in the most northerly areas of Russia, and these will cause further melting of some of the permafrost, which will fundamentally affect the biodiversity of animal and plant species in local ecosystems. The arctic tundra vegetation of the northern areas is expected to be forced northward and to be partially replaced by taiga forest cover extending its range from the south. The melting of permafrost is also likely to cause increased damage to infrastructure such as roads, pipelines, and buildings, and this process is already being observed along the Arctic Ocean coastal fringe of Russia.

Warmer temperatures will also melt sea ice and reduce sea ice cover in winter, which may allow better transportation links across the sea. Melting of glaciers is also expected, with both positive and negative implications, such as increased hydroelectricity capacity but also increased flood risk.

The change in climate is expected to result in increased precipitation over the next one hundred years, which may also increase flood risk in low-lying areas with heavy rainfall. Average sea levels are expected to rise, so that populations in the low-lying urban coastal areas will be at increased risk from flooding.

M. FELTON

CLIMATE

IRKUTSK, RUSSIAN FEDERATION

52°16'N 104°23'E   Height above sea level 1,676 feet (511 m)

	J	F	M	A	M	J	J	A	S	O	N	D
						Mean maximum						
(°F)	3	10	25	43	55	68	70	68	57	41	19	3
(°C)	-16	-12	-4	6	13	20	21	20	14	5	-7	-16
						Mean minimum						
(°F)	-15	-13	1	19	34	45	50	48	36	21	1	-11
(°C)	-26	-25	-17	-7	1	7	10	9	2	-6	-17	-24
						Precipitation						
(in.)	0.5	0.4	0.3	0.6	1.3	2.2	3.1	2.8	1.7	0.7	0.6	0.6
(cm)	1.3	1.0	0.8	1.5	3.3	5.6	7.9	7.1	4.3	1.8	1.5	1.5

MOSCOW, RUSSIAN FEDERATION

55°24'N 37°54'E   Height above sea level 623 feet (190 m)

	J	F	M	A	M	J	J	A	S	O	N	D
						Mean maximum						
(°F)	16	21	32	50	66	70	73	72	61	48	36	23
(°C)	-9	-6	0	10	19	21	23	22	16	9	2	-5
						Mean minimum						
(°F)	3	7	18	34	46	52	55	54	45	37	27	14
(°C)	-16	-14	-8	1	8	11	13	12	7	3	-3	-10
						Precipitation						
(in.)	1.5	1.5	1.4	1.5	2.1	2.3	3.5	2.8	2.3	1.8	1.9	2.1
(cm)	3.9	3.8	3.6	3.7	5.3	5.8	8.8	7.1	5.8	4.5	4.7	5.4

SOCHI, RUSSIAN FEDERATION

43°35'N 39°40'E   Height above sea level 10 feet (3 m)

	J	F	M	A	M	J	J	A	S	O	N	D
						Mean maximum						
(°F)	50	50	55	61	70	75	79	81	77	68	63	55
(°C)	10	10	13	16	21	24	26	27	25	20	17	13
						Mean minimum						
(°F)	37	39	41	48	55	61	66	66	61	54	50	43
(°C)	3	4	5	9	13	16	19	19	16	12	10	6
						Precipitation						
(in.)	7.9	5.0	5.1	4.6	3.7	4.0	2.4	4.0	4.2	3.6	5.6	7.2
(cm)	20.1	12.6	13.0	11.6	9.3	10.1	6.0	10.1	10.6	9.1	14.3	18.3

Flora and Fauna of Belarus, Russia, and Ukraine

The region of Russia, Belarus, and Ukraine occupies a huge area, stretching from central Europe to the Bering Strait and deep into Central Asia. Within this area, there is a wide diversity of habitats.

Stretching over a broad range of latitude and longitude and combining oceanic and continental climates, the region formed by Belarus, Russia, and Ukraine has an enormous diversity of vegetation and animal populations. It is estimated that the region is home to about 13,000 species of vascular plants (higher plants), 130,000 species of invertebrates, and 1,300 species of vertebrates.

Worldwide, there are two main patterns in distribution of vegetation cover: zonality and vertical differentiation, which overlap and supplement each other. Zonality (or latitudinal differentiation) is the climate-determined progressive change of vegetation from the poles to the Equator. This division is very distinct across the vast expanses of Russia, where, from north to south, there are zones of arctic ice cover, tundra, forest-tundra, taiga, mixed forests, broad-leaved forests, forest-steppe, steppe, and desert, each in a broadly east-west band. Mediterranean forests line the Black Sea coast, protected by the Crimean and Caucasus mountains from the cold Arctic air.

A similar pattern of habitats is exhibited vertically, with arctic-type zones at mountaintops, and, descending, alpine meadows, zones of stunted trees, coniferous forests, and mixed woodland. Although these vegetation belts in high mountains are similar to the latitudinal zones, vertical differentiation in each mountain range is more patchy, and differences depend on height, location, local climate, slope, aspect, and physical conditions of surrounding plains.

THE TUNDRA

Tundra is a treeless region, which stretches along the entire Arctic coast of Russia. There is no prevailing life-form in tundra flora, which is a combination of dwarf shrubs, low perennial herbs, mosses, and lichens. Common features of these plants are tolerance to very low temperatures and a low growth form, which allows them to be protected by snow cover in winter. Plant height, productivity, and biodiversity increase in the tundra region toward the south. Mountain avens and some grasses and sedges dominate in tundra plant communities together with dwarf shrubs, such as cranberries, bog blueberries, and crowberries. In the southern tundra, slightly higher temperatures allow some small trees, including dwarf birches, downy willows, Siberian dwarf pines, and Siberian alders.

Reindeer moss, a favorite food of reindeer, is the best-known lichen species of the tundra.

The animals of the tundra are more diverse than the flora. Polar foxes, lemmings, and (almost completely domesticated) reindeer are the most typical mammals of the Russian tundra. Numerous birds in the region include snowy owls, ptarmigans, rough-legged buzzards, Bewick's swans, king eiders, and many others, which breed in the tundra in the short summer, when plant growth and the hatching of many insects provide food.

Remote, inaccessible arctic coasts provide nesting grounds for huge colonies of arctic terns, guillemots, little auks, and other birds. The waters of the Arctic Ocean are home to seals and walruses, as well as many fish. The remote arctic islands and seasonal pack ice are inhabited by polar bears, whose future is endangered by rising temperatures and melting ice.

THE FOREST-TUNDRA ZONE

The thinly wooded forest-tundra zone is transitional between the arctic tundra to the north and wooded taiga to the south. Forest-tundra has the appearance of stunted, open woodland, where scattered trees, such as Norway firs and larches, stand among tundra plant communities and peat bogs. The small, stunted trees are widely spaced. Shallow roots are concentrated in the upper

Siberian tigers are an endangered species; many animals are protected, such as this one in a game park.

The town of Suzdal, which dates to 1024, was sacked by the Mongols in 1238, during their invasion of Russia.

Hungary. However, strong resistance from the Czechs forced the invaders to withdraw eastward to the steppes. As a result of these invasions, about half of the Russian population perished and large cities were completely destroyed. Socially, culturally, and economically, the development of Russia was set back.

THE GOLDEN HORDE

The Russian lands were then subject to a new state, known as the Golden Horde, which was founded by the Tatars along the lower Volga River. From its national capital, Sarai (which became one of the largest cities of the medieval world), the khan, ruler of the Tatars, controlled the areas that are now European Russia, Ukraine, and some of the Caucasian region, although he was (initially, in theory) subject to the huge Mongol empire.

The Tatars did not establish formal dominion over the Russian princes, who were allowed to reign but had to submit to the khan. After the death of Yuri II of Vladimir, his brother Yaroslav II (1191–1246; reigned 1238–1246) journeyed to the Golden Horde to gain permission (*yarlyk*) to succeed in Vladimir in 1243. Other princes also had to go the khan to confirm their right to reign. In 1257–1259, the Tatars conducted a census, and all adults recorded had to pay tribute to them. Besides this tribute, the Russians had to pay 14 other taxes to the Tatars, which were collected by *baskaks* (tax collectors). Russian cities also had to supply artisans and military personnel to the Golden Horde. To maintain control, the Tatars organized punitive campaigns, which kept the people in fear.

THE STRUGGLE FOR INDEPENDENCE

During the fourteenth century, the Tatars devastated most of Russia, but, at the same time, the struggle for independence started in the major Russian city-states. The system of *baskaks* was abandoned, and Russian princes began to collect the tribute and bring it to the khan themselves.

In the middle of the fourteenth century, the principal challenge to Tatar rule came not from formerly great cities, such as Kiev, Vladimir, and Novgorod, but from Moscow. The effective power of the Tatars had been waning, as a result of civil war and dynastic disputes after the assassination of the last legitimate khan, Berdi Beg (reigned 1357–1359). The grand prince of Moscow, Dmitri I Ivanovich (Dimitri Donskoi; 1350–1389; reigned 1359–1389), had already gained ascendancy over other princes in northern Russia, and his reconstruction of a fortress (known as the Kremlin), strong enough to resist invasion by the Lithuanians, gave him confidence to challenge the Tatars. In 1378, Mamai (died 1380), a Mongol-Tatar general and one of the claimants to the throne of the Golden Horde, attempted to impose taxation on the Russian princes and sent an army against Dmitri, whom he perceived was becoming too powerful. However, Mamai was defeated by Dmitri in the battle of the Vozha River.

At the battle of Kulikovo in September 1380, Mamai's army was completely defeated by Muscovite forces. This battle, which strengthened the prestige of Moscow as the center of Russia, is regarded as a turning point in Russian history. The power of the Golden Horde appeared broken and, two years after the victory, the Russian princes ceased to pay tribute to the Golden Horde. However, in 1382, a new strong khan was installed in the Golden Horde, Tokhtamysh (died 1406), who captured and burned Moscow. As a result, Dmitri started to pay tribute again, but, by the beginning of the fifteenth century, allegiance to the Tatar ruler was nominal.

K. VOZDIGAN

The Rise of Moscow

Expanding from the fourteenth century, the grand principality, or grand duchy, of Moscow became the core around which Russia was to be built. By the middle of the sixteenth century, its sovereign ruled an empire and took the title "czar."

The city of Moscow was founded in the mid-twelfth century by people from the city of Yaroslavl. In 1263, Daniel (1261–1303; reigned 1263–1303), youngest son of Alexander I (Alexander Nevsky; c. 1220–1263; reigned as prince of Novgorod 1238–1252 and as prince of Novgorod and Vladimir 1252–1263), was given his father's smallest domain, Moscow. This principality covered only some 15 square miles (about 40 sq. km), but was along the Moscow River, a tributary of the Oka River, which, in turn, flows to the Volga, a major trade route.

Daniel ruled peacefully, avoiding the almost constant wars between the Russian princes. However, he extended his small state, gaining the city of Kolomna by a ruse, and was bequeathed Pereslavl and Zalessky. As a result, Daniel controlled a strategic location in the region. Like other Russian rulers, his son, Ivan I Kalita (1288–1340), was a subject of the Tatar khan, the monarch of the Golden Horde (a state along the lower Volga River), to whom he had to pay tribute. Ivan received permission from the Golden Horde to be the only collector of tribute in the region, and, consequently, Ivan not only managed to deliver the taxes but also amassed a fortune for himself, greatly strengthening the grand principality of Moscow.

DMITRI DONSKOI

During the rule of Ivan's grandson, Dmitri I Ivanovich (Dmitri Donskoi; 1350–1389; reigned 1359–1389), the princes of the Russian cities joined forces against the army of the Golden Horde. The Tatars were bitterly divided in a civil war, following the death of the khan in 1359. As a result, they were gravely weakened. Mamai (died 1380), a Mongol-Tatar general who was one of the claimants to the throne of the Golden Horde, attempted to impose taxes on the Russian princes. Dmitri had already gained ascendancy over other princes in northern Russia, and, when Mamai sent an army against him, Dmitri felt confident enough to resist. Dmitri defeated Mamai in the battle of the Vozha River (1378). Then, two years later, an army of some 100,000 people, commanded by Dmitri, set out against Mamai.

The decisive battle took place near the Don River on the Kulikovo Field. The army of the Golden Horde was defeated, but Mamai escaped. Dmitri, who became known as Dmitri Donskoi, meaning "Dmitri of the Don," returned to Moscow as unquestioned leader of the Russian princes. However, in 1382, Mongol leader Tokhtamysh (died 1406), who had replaced Mamai, suddenly launched a new invasion on the Russian lands.

In spite of fierce resistance by Dmitri's army, the city of Moscow was almost destroyed by the Mongol-Tatars. Subsequently, the Russian princes remained subject to the Tatars and continued paying tribute.

INVASIONS FROM THE EAST

The battle on Kulikovo Field revealed the necessity for cooperation of the Russian states and the need for a single strong leader to defeat the Mongol-Tatars. However, Russia was still too weak and disunited to resist invasions. In 1395, Tokhtamysh was overthrown by Mongol conqueror Timur (formerly known as Tamerlane; 1336–1405), who ruled an empire that covered Central Asia, the Caucasus region, and modern-day Iran, Iraq, and Afghanistan. Timur began a new invasion of Russia, and Vasily I (1371–1425; reigned 1389–1425), son of Dmitri Donskoi, set out against this powerful enemy, who returned to the steppes without giving battle. Vasily then felt strong enough to stop paying tribute, but he continued to collect these taxes, thereby enriching his treasury and providing money for arms and military personnel.

In 1408, Tatar khan Edigu or Edigei (1352–1419) ravaged the region near Moscow, demanded and collected a heavy tribute, and then returned to the steppes. After constant battles, Moscow was still too weak to resist new invasions. During the reign of Vasily II (1415–1462; reigned 1425–1462), Moscow suffered prolonged civil war, involving constant conflicts between the descendants of Dmitri Donskoi. Consequently, the Muscovite state was weak; although the Golden Horde broke up into smaller khanates, the Tatar threat was not removed. The Kazan khanate became strong, and its ruler Olug Moxammat (died 1445) besieged Moscow. In 1445, Olug Moxammat took Vasily prisoner and held him for ransom.

TERRITORIAL EXPANSION

After the death of Vasily II, his elder son, Ivan III (1440–1505; reigned 1462–1503), proved a stronger ruler. He not only managed to remain on the throne but also greatly extended the state. Ivan successfully conducted a war against the Republic of Novgorod in 1481, forcing Novgorod to cede much territory to Moscow. In 1478, he made Novgorod recognize him as sovereign, and thus acquired the city and its large possessions. Ivan added

The guiding principles of Russian foreign policy at the time was stability and nonintervention in European political affairs. Alexander III prioritized the national interests of Russia, and he gained the nickname "the Peacemaker," because there were no serious military operations during his reign.

NICHOLAS II

The last emperor, Nicholas II (1868–1918; reigned 1894–1917), did not have the ability to confront the many problems facing Russia, and he was also kept almost a recluse by the security forces. Nicholas was influenced by his unpopular German wife, Alexandra (1872–1918). She, in turn, was increasingly guided by Grigori Rasputin (1869–1916), a debauched religious mystic who seemed able to bring some relief to the imperial couple's only son, who was a hemophiliac.

In January 1904, the Japanese navy attacked Port Arthur (now Dalien, China), which was the main Russian strategic base in eastern Asia. Despite strong resistance by the Russian army and navy, in May 1905 the Japanese won the Battle of Zusima Channel. In August, Russia acknowledged defeat, signing a peace treaty under which it had to acknowledge Japanese interests in Korea and to cede southern Sakhalin to Japan. Defeat at the hands of Japan had serious consequences for the imperial regime, influencing the internal political crisis in Russia in 1905.

Nicholas advocated autocracy, but he also realized the necessity of the capitalist development of the state. Discontent was widespread, and, in the first years of the twentieth century, revolutionary organizations again surfaced in Russia. In January 1905, a huge demonstration of protesters, led by a priest, Georgiy Gapon (1870–1906), peacefully marched through Saint Petersburg, then the Russian national capital, bringing a petition to the emperor, asking for reforms. Army units fired on the petitioners, killing many—although the authorities claimed that only 96 had died. The incident, known to history as Bloody Sunday, led to the 1905 revolution and undermined support for Nicholas.

THE 1905 REVOLUTION

In February 1905, more than 800,000 workers and peasants went on strike across Russia. In several provinces, peasants seized the estates and food stores of their landlords. The government suppressed local uprisings by force. However, more people, especially students and members of the intelligentsia, joined revolutionary organizations. In the summer of 1905, army and navy units mutinied in Sevastopol, Kronstadt (near Saint Petersburg), and Vladivostok.

In October 1905, Moscow became the main center of the strikes, although some 120 cities were involved, with more than two million people on strike. Railroads, urban transportation, and water utilities did not work; drug stores, post offices, and the state bank were closed. In Saint Petersburg, police managed to

Undated engraving of Nicholas I (reigned 1825–1855).

assassinated in a bomb explosion in Saint Petersburg. The brief experiment with cautious reform and democratization died with Alexander II.

ALEXANDER III

Alexander III (1845–1894; reigned 1881–1894), the eldest surviving son of Alexander II, rejected the liberal policies of his father. The new emperor strove to strengthen autocracy and forbade further discussion about reform. He reconsidered his father's legal reforms and the changes that Alexander II had made to administrative institutions. Consequently, the emperor increased his hold on government, the judiciary, and all aspects of administration. Alexander III reestablished an absolute monarchy, and, with increased repression, the activities of numerous revolutionary organizations were suppressed, and no further terrorist attacks were attempted.

Although political repression intensified, economic progress was made. Financial support was available to landowners, and a program was established to encourage peasants to take credit to redeem their land from landlords. At the same time, the government launched resettlement programs in Siberia and Central Asia, most of which had by then come under Russian rule.

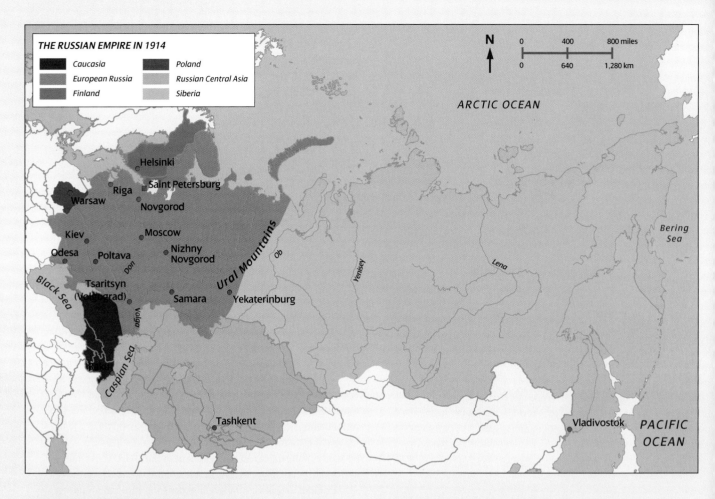

THE RUSSIAN EMPIRE IN 1914

- Caucasia
- European Russia
- Finland
- Poland
- Russian Central Asia
- Siberia

prevent armed revolt, and many leaders of local rebel groups were captured. Armed forces, loyal to the emperor and the regime, were transferred to Moscow, and, in December 1905, the rebellion there was quashed.

LIMITED REFORMS

Reform was now inevitable. The emperor signed the Manifest, a document guaranteeing civil rights, freedom of speech, and freedom of assembly. A new legislative body, the State Duma, was established, although the emperor retained the right to approve laws and dissolve the Duma before the end of its five-year term. The armed forces and the government were still in the hands of the emperor, and Russia was far from being a democracy.

The first political parties appeared in Russia before 1905. Their leaders mostly came from the intelligentsia and advocated national and socialist ideas. Liberal and conservative parties were also formed after the strikes of 1905. The Social-Democratic Party advocated socialism, an end to the monarchy, and the establishment of a democratic republic with universal suffrage. Liberal ideas featured in the program of the Constitutional-Democratic Party, whose aim was constitutional government, either monarchical or republican. There were also several political groups supporting the autocracy.

From 1906, the authorities gave much attention to army reforms. The development of the defense industry became urgent as international tension increased in Europe. In 1914, World War I (1914–1918) began, with Russia in alliance with Great Britain and France against Germany and Austria-Hungary. The military campaigns of 1914–1915 were successful, but, by 1916, the tide of the war turned against Russia. The Russian army had heavy casualties, and opposition to the war grew. The government supported the defense industry more than any other branch of production. Nevertheless, Russian forces lacked sufficient weapons.

In 1916, the price of consumer commodities steeply rose, as industrial production focused on defense. Inflation increased and food shortages were experienced, while families became alarmed by stories of many Russian casualties on the front. As a result, in February 1917, workers in Moscow and Saint Petersburg declared a strike, initially with economic demands. Later in the month, the strike turned into full-scale rebellion with political demands, including the abolition of the autocracy. The emperor ordered the army to quell the rebels, but many soldiers joined workers on strike. Nicolas II dissolved the State Duma, and the liberals lost the last opportunity to establish a constitutional monarchy. Only a revolution could now bring change.

For subsequent history, see pages 1343, 1361–1372, and 1421.

O. BOGDANOVA

The Peoples of Belarus, Russia, and Ukraine

The Russian Federation and, to a lesser extent, Ukraine and Belarus are characterized by great ethnic diversity. In Russia, this diversity is reflected in a number of autonomous republics and other self-governing territories established for different minorities.

Ethnic Russians account for 80 percent of the population of the Russian Federation. The remaining 20 percent comprises other Europeans, including Ukrainians, Chechens, Armenians, Belarussians (also given as Belarusians), Germans, Ossetians, Moldovans, and other Caucasian peoples; Turkic peoples, such as Tatars, Bashkirs, Chuvash people, Kazakhs, Azeris, Yakuts, and others; and Asian peoples such as Buryats, Koreans, Mongols, and Yakuts.

RUSSIANS

As well as forming the overwhelming majority of the population of the Russian Federation, Russians were widespread across the former territories of the nineteenth-century Russian Empire and the twentieth-century Soviet Union. Russians are a minority in other former Soviet republics, accounting for 17 percent of the population of Ukraine by ethnicity and 24 percent by language. In Belarus, ethnic Russians account for 11 percent of the republic's population.

The Russian heartland was the region around the Dnieper and Volga rivers, which accepted Orthodox Christianity from the tenth century. From this region, partly in modern Russia and partly in modern Ukraine, the Christianization and Russification of territories to the north and east began. In this process, various Finno-Ugrian peoples were Russified. This process of Russification continued through centuries as various other peoples were absorbed; others, however, remained distinct in language, customs, and society, and, sometimes, also in religion.

The Russian Orthodox Church was an agent of Russification, and its structures and practices spread across the former Russian Empire. Today, some 16 percent of the population of Russia practice their Orthodox beliefs, although around 70 percent of the population identifies with the Orthodox culture. At the same time, 65–70 percent of the population of Russia is nonreligious.

While Russians and their religion spread across their empire, other peoples moved within it. The Soviet period in particular witnessed widespread migration, including the exile of large numbers of people to Siberia and the inflow of Central Asian and Transcaucasian economic migrants to Russian cities. Although Ukraine and Belarus received smaller numbers of migrants, they too became multinational with representatives of nearly all the ethnic groups of the former Soviet Union. In modern times, some ethnic Russians have moved back to Russia from Central Asian and other republics that are now independent, although Asiatic and Turkic peoples, as well as Georgians and Armenians, still work in larger Russian cities in considerable numbers.

Outside Russia, ethnic Russians are most prominent in the cities of Belarus and Ukraine, particularly in the regions that are sometimes called Novorossia or new Ukraine—the Odesa, Kherson, and Crimean regions. There are also many Russians in the industrial Donbas (or Donets Basin) region of eastern Ukraine. Eastern Ukraine has a significant Russian population, and its ethnic Ukrainian population is also Russian speaking.

UKRAINIANS AND BELARUSSIANS

Ethnic Ukrainians account for some 78 percent of the population of Ukraine, although only 67 percent of the population speak Ukrainian as a first language. Ukrainians also form some 2 percent of the population of Russia and around 2 percent of that of Belarus. Ukrainians are, like Russians, an East Slavic people and are also Orthodox Christians. Although 25 percent of the population of Ukraine belong to three different Orthodox churches, at least 38 percent are nonreligious (atheists and agnostics), and around 21 percent follow no religious practice.

The Belarussians, also East Slavs, make up 81 percent of the population of Belarus. Belarussians are also a small minority in northwestern Ukraine and western Russia. Some 40–45 percent of Belarussians belong to the Russian Orthodox tradition, although fewer than 8 percent are practicing. The Belarussian identity is, to some extent, modern and is based on the language and culture of the people which, until the nineteenth century, was largely confined to the rural poor.

EUROPEAN MINORITIES

Belarus, Russia, and Ukraine are home to various European minorities. Poles form 4 percent of the population of Belarus, much of which was part of Poland until 1945. Poles are also a minority in Ukraine, where Lviv was a Polish city until 1945. Ukraine also has minorities of Moldovans (Romanians), Bulgarians, and Hungarians in the west and Ruthenians in the Transcarpathia region.

Russia's European minorities are larger. They include Germans, a small minority of whom descend from the Baltic Germans who settled along the Baltic coasts of what are now Estonia, Latvia, and Lithuania from the twelfth and thirteenth centuries. The majority, however, descend from later groups of Germans who were encouraged to settle in Russia for commercial reasons.

Chechens, from the Caucasus, account for 1 percent of the Russian population. In modern times, a Chechen separatist movement resulted in a Chechen declaration of independence (1991) and two wars with Russia. The second Chechen war (1999) brought the restoration of Russian authority over Chechnya and the installation of a pro-Russian government. The Chechen conflict, however, is not merely ethnic but is partly rooted in disputes between Chechen clans (*tape*) and by the division between Sufis and Wahhabis of the Muslim Chechen population. Chechens in Russia live not only in Chechnya, neighboring Dagestan, and other parts of the Caucasus but also in Moscow, where the involvement of Chechens, as well as people from Dagestan and Azeris, in criminal activity and their control over grocery stores and fruit markets in Russia led to widespread hostility toward people from the southern Caucasus.

Armenians and Georgians, also from the Caucasus, are significant minorities in Russia, in the region immediately north of the Caucasus Mountains and also in Russia's major cities. The Caucasus is an ethnic jigsaw with many different minorities. The autonomous republic of Dagestan is particularly rich in ethnic groups and cultures, including the Avars, but also is prone to ethnic conflict owing to differences in interest of the various groups. Land ownership was the main reason for some disputes of the 1990s, when Russia faced a number of conflicts in the north Caucasus region. Some had roots in the imperial past of Russia; others are the heritage of the Soviet Union of Joseph Stalin (1879–1953; leader of the Soviet Communist Party and effectively ruler of Russia 1922–1953). The Ossetians and Ingush, in the North Ossetia (or Alania) autonomous republic, contested land initially owned by the Ingush but that was taken by the Ossetians after Stalin expelled the Ingush to Central Asia. The Kabardins, of the autonomous republic of Kabardino-Balkaria, are a Muslim Caucasian people from the same region.

The Karelians, in the northwest adjoining Finland, are a Baltic-Finnish people who are closely related to the Finns. Their region, along Lake Ladoga, was part of Finland before World War II (1939–1945) but was annexed by the Soviet Union after war with Finland. The Karelians are so close to the Finns, in culture and ethnicity, that the Karelian population in eastern Finland has been assimilated into the Finnish population. The Mordvins, another Finno-Ugric group, mainly live in the autonomous republic of Mordovia, while the related Mari people have their own autonomous republic, Mariy-El.

TURKIC PEOPLES

Turkic peoples in Russia, and to a lesser extent in Ukraine, are either the descendants of Tatar invaders from the east in the Middle Ages or peoples whose homelands were overrun by the Russians in the eastward expansion of the Russian Empire. The

Devotional objects in the tent of a Kalmyk nomad.

Traditional Ukrainian dress is now most commonly worn for folk dances.

southern parts of present-day Ukraine and Russia were subject to Turkic invasions from the sixth century CE. Many Turkic-speaking groups settled in Ukraine and the Volga region. Later, the Mongols brought with them subordinate Turkic groups, including the Tatars. The acceptance of Islam by the ruler of the Tatar state known as the Golden Horde, in the thirteenth century, increased the Islamization of the Volga region. The grand principality of Moscow conquered the Volga khanates in the sixteenth century, and local Muslims were incorporated into Russia. Many abandoned Islam and became Russified.

In modern times, the Volga region contains a number of ethnic autonomous republics that are home to various, mainly Turkic, peoples. The largest ethnic group is the Tatars, who account for 4 percent of the population of Russia. The Tatar homeland, Tatarstan, contains the large city of Kazan. Some 49 percent of the population of the autonomous republic of Tatarstan are Tatar and 44 percent are ethnically Russian. Historically, Tatars also referred to Mongol invaders of Russia, and there is considerable ethnic diversity among modern Tatars, although the majority of the Volga Tatars are Caucasian. There are also Crimean Tatars, whose entire

population was expelled from their homeland to Central Asia by Stalin, who accused them of collaboration with Germany in World War II. The Crimean Tatars returned to Crimea after the independence of Ukraine in 1991. Further groups of Tatars, who are more Asiatic, live in communities in Siberia. Tatars include Sunni Muslims and Orthodox Christians, although the majority are nonreligious.

The Bashkirs are a Turkic people, who speak their own language and Russian and who are mainly Sunni Muslims. They live in the autonomous republic of Bashkortostan, although some also live in Tatarstan. In Bashkortostan, Bashkirs form only 22 percent of the republic's population, a smaller percentage than ethnic Russians or Tatars.

Kazakhs are a substantial minority in regions bordering independent Kazakhstan, while Chuvash people, who account for 1 percent of the Russian population, mainly live in or near the autonomous Chuvash Republic (or Chuvashia), which is in the Volga region. The Chuvash people, who speak their own language and retain some pre-Christian customs, form two-thirds of the population of Chuvashia and also live in Tatarstan and Bashkortostan. The majority are Orthodox Christians. Yakuts form a minority, some 36 percent of the population, in the huge east Siberian autonomous republic of Sakha. A Turkic people, they speak Sakha, and some still follow traditional religions based on shamanism (shamans are priest-healers).

ASIAN PEOPLES

Mongol invasions of European Russia through the Middle Ages brought Mongol and other peoples into the region. Later, as the Russian Empire extended into Asia, various Asian peoples came under Russian rule. Although some of those peoples were granted Union republics—republics equal in status with Russia within the Soviet Union—and subsequently obtained independence in 1991 when the Soviet Union collapsed, other Asian peoples remain within the Russian Federation.

Mongols live in a wide area along border regions with Mongolia. The Buryats, who have their own autonomous republic (Buryatia), are the largest ethnic minority in Siberia. They are a Mongol people, many of whom still follow Tibetan Buddhism. Kalmyks, who live in the autonomous republic of Kalmykia, are a western Mongolian people who migrated from Central Asia in the seventeenth century to the western shores of the Caspian Sea. Many are still Buddhists. Tuvans inhabit a small region along the border with Mongolia. This Buddhist Mongol people formed their own independent state, Tannu Tuva, from 1921 through 1944, when it was annexed by the Soviet Union.

Russia's Korean population is different from other Asiatic populations in the Russian Federation. They are the descendants of economic migrants who settled in the eastern parts of Siberia from the 1860s.

I. KOTIN

Belarus

Belarus became a sovereign nation upon the collapse of the Soviet Union in 1991; previously, it had been the Belorussian Soviet Socialist Republic (SSR). From the Middle Ages, the region, home to the Belarussians (also given as Belarusians), or White Russians, was part of Lithuania and, from 1569, part of Poland-Lithuania. In the three partitions of Poland (1772, 1793, and 1795), the region was annexed by Russia. The Belorussian lands were the scene of heavy fighting during World War I (1914–1918) and, in 1919, much of the region was invaded by Poland, while a Soviet republic was established in the east. From 1919 through 1991, the region was a Communist republic, from 1922 part of the Soviet Union. Much of the Belorussian SSR was devastated during World War II (1939–1945), when German forces occupied the region, most of whose Jewish population was killed in German concentration camps. Because of the 1986 Chernobyl nuclear power station accident in neighboring Ukraine, some areas of the south had to be abandoned, and an unknown number of people developed cancers. Since independence, under the name Belarus, the country has remained a Soviet-style dictatorship.

GEOGRAPHY

Location	Eastern Europe, between Poland and the Russian Federation
Climate	Cold, snowy winters; cool, moist summers
Area	80,134 sq. miles (207,546 sq. km)
Coastline	Landlocked
Highest point	Dzyarzhynskaya 1,135 feet (346 m)
Lowest point	Neman River 295 feet (90 m)
Terrain	Largely flat; marshy in the south; the low Belorussian Ridge runs east to west through the center of the country
Natural resources	Peat, building materials, potassium, potash, lignite, salt
Land use	
Arable land	26.8 percent
Permanent crops	0.6 percent
Other	72.6 percent
Major rivers	Western Dvina (Daugava), Neman, Pripyat, Dnieper
Major lakes	Narach (also given as Naroch)
Natural hazards	Floods

METROPOLITAN AREAS, 2005 POPULATION

Urban population	73 percent
Minsk	1,766,000
Homyel' (Homel; formerly Gomel)	481,000
Mahilyow (formerly Mogilev)	367,000
Vitsyebsk (formerly Vitebsk)	343,000
Hrodna (Hrodno; formerly Grodno)	317,000
Brest	300,000
Babruysk (Bobruysk)	220,000
Baranavichy (Baranovichi)	168,000
Barysaw (formerly Borisov)	150,000
Pinsk	130,000
Orsha (Vorsha)	125,000
Mazyr (formerly Mozyr)	112,000
Salihorsk (formerly Soligorsk)	101,000
Navapolatsk (formerly Novopolock)	101,000

Source: Belarussian government estimates, 2005. In modern times, more than one transliteration of Belarussian names is used; the most common version is given above. Other frequently used spellings and former Russian names, which are also still widely used, are given in brackets.

NEIGHBORS AND LENGTH OF BORDERS

Latvia	106 miles (171 km)
Lithuania	423 miles (680 km)
Poland	376 miles (605 km)
Russian Federation	596 miles (959 km)
Ukraine	554 miles (891 km)

POPULATION

Population	9,751,000 (2005 government estimate)
Population density	122 per sq. mile (47 per sq. km)
Population growth	-0.4 percent a year
Birthrate	9.6 births per 1,000 of the population

Death rate	13.9 deaths per 1,000 of the population
Population under age 15	14.4 percent
Population over age 65	14.7 percent
Sex ratio	106 males for 100 females
Fertility rate	1.2 children per woman
Infant mortality rate	6.5 deaths per 1,000 live births
Life expectancy at birth	
Total population	70.3 years
Female	76.4 years
Male	64.6 years

ECONOMY

Currency	Belarussian ruble (BYR)
Exchange rate (2008)	$1 = BYR 2,142
Gross domestic product (2007)	$103.5 billion
GDP per capita (2007)	$10,600
Unemployment rate (2005)	1.6 percent; many underemployed
Population under poverty line (2003)	27.1 percent
Exports	$24.4 billion (2007 CIA estimate)
Imports	$28.3 billion (2007 CIA estimate)

GOVERNMENT

Official country name	Republic of Belarus
Conventional short form	Belarus
Former names	Belorussian Soviet Socialist Republic; Byelorussia

FLAG

Except for the absence of the hammer and sickle emblem, the flag of Belarus (adopted in 1995) is a version of that flown when the country was the Belorussian Soviet Socialist Republic. The field (background) is red to represent the Soviet Red Army, which liberated the region from Nazi German occupation. There is a horizontal green stripe along the base, representing hope and the future. In the hoist (the side next to the flagpole) is a vertical decorative bar, in white and red, representing traditional folk art.

The cathedral of Saint Francis Xavier, in Hrodna, was originally built as a Jesuit church in 1678.

Nationality

noun	Belarussian or Belarusian
adjective	Belarussian or Belarusian
Official languages	Belarussian, Russian
Capital city	Minsk
Type of government	Presidential republic; dictatorship
Voting rights	18 years, universal
National anthem	"My Belarusy" (We Belarussians)
National day	Independence Day, July 3 (1944; anniversary of the liberation of Minsk in World War II; the actual date of independence from the Soviet Union was August 25, 1991)

TRANSPORTATION

Railroads	3,426 miles (5,512 km)
Highways	58,904 miles (94,797 km)
Paved roads	52,213 miles (84,028 km)
Unpaved roads	6,693 miles (10,769 km)
Navigable waterways	1,554 miles (2,500 km); little used commercially
Airports	
International airports	1
Paved runways	36

POPULATION PROFILE, 2007 ESTIMATES

Ethnic groups

Europeans	virtually 100 percent (of which Belarussians form 81 percent; Russians 11 percent; Poles 4 percent; Ukrainians 2 percent; others 2 percent)

Religions

Russian Orthodox	40-45 percent; fewer than 8 percent practicing
Autocephalous Belarussian Orthodox Church*	unknown
Roman Catholic	10 percent; 5 percent practicing
Belarussian Greek Catholic Church	1 percent
Baptists, Seventh-Day Adventists, Evangelical Christians, Old Believers, Lutherans, and other Christians	2 percent
Jewish, Sunni Islam, and others	1 percent
Nonreligious	more than 35 percent

* Subject to active persecution

Languages

Belarussian	81 percent as a first language
Russian	12 percent as a first language but almost universally understood
Polish	4 percent
Ukrainian	2 percent
Others	1 percent
Adult literacy	over 99 percent

CHRONOLOGY

6th century CE	Slavs settle the region that is now Belarus.
mid-9th century CE	The region comes under the control of the Kievan Rus principality to the south. Scandinavian Vikings establish trading posts along the region's main waterways.
9th–12th century	Most of what is now Belarus is included in the principality of Polatsk.
13th century	Mongol invasions topple Kievan Rus and Polatsk, and the region that is now Belarus becomes part of Lithuania.
1486	Russia begins attempts to wrest control of the region from Lithuania.
1569	Poland and Lithuania enter a formal union, the Commonwealth of Poland and Lithuania.
1772, 1793, and 1795	In the three partitions of Poland, the region is annexed to Russia and generally becomes known as White Russia.
1914–1918	White Russia is the scene of heavy fighting during World War I, as German forces push back the Russian imperial army.
1918–1919	White Russian (Belorussian) nationalists declare independence in 1918, but, in 1919, the Polish army invades Belorussia from the west, while Soviet Russian troops invade from the east. A Communist republic is established.
1921	Poland and the Soviet Union divide Belorussia between them.
1922	The Belorussian Soviet Socialist Republic (SSR) becomes a constituent member of the Soviet Union.
1941–1944	In World War II (1939–1945), Nazi Germany invades and occupies the Belorussian SSR. Most of the republic's substantial Jewish population are deported to German concentration camps and are murdered. Around 2.2 million Belorussians die in the war.
1945	Western Belorussia is ceded by Poland to the Soviet Union and is merged with the Belorussian SSR.
1986	Fallout from the Chernobyl nuclear power station in neighboring Ukraine affects southern Belorussia. Many people later develop cancers, and a region in the south has to be abandoned for agriculture and settlement.
1991	The Soviet Union collapses, and the Belorussian SSR becomes the republic of Belarus. However, the country does not dismantle its Soviet-era governmental or economic systems.
1994	Alexander Lukashenko (born 1954) becomes president. He begins to establish a dictatorship.
1995–2000	Belarus draws closer to Russia, proposing a new union between the countries.
2006 and 2007	Demonstrators protest flawed elections; opposition figures are detained.

CULTURAL EXPRESSION

The culture of Belarus has been shaped by various factors, including the early influence of Balts and Scandinavians; an East Slavic heritage; the sharing of a state with the Lithuanians from the fourteenth century; the significant influence of Jewish culture; Polish and then Russian rule; the devastation of World War II (1939–1945); and the Soviet era (1919–1941 and 1944–1991).

The Old Belarussian (also given as Belarusian) language emerged in the thirteenth century from the East Slavic language. The foundations of literary Old Belarussian were laid by Italian-educated scholar and poet Francis Skaryna (1485–1540), who printed the first book in Old Belarussian in 1517. Old Belarussian, written in Cyrillic script, was an official language of medieval Lithuania, but when, in 1569, Lithuania became part of the Polish-Lithuanian Commonwealth, Polish, a Slavic language written in the Latin script, replaced Old Belarussian as the official language. In the late eighteenth century, the Belarussian lands were annexed by Russia, and Russian, a Slavic language written in the Cyrillic script, succeeded Polish as the official language. Because the nobility adopted either Polish or Russian, Old Belarussian was then spoken only among the peasants and the poorer people.

LITERATURE

Formal literature based on modern Belarussian developed during the national revival of the nineteenth century, thanks to the literary efforts of Polish-educated landed gentry such as Jan Czeczot (1796–1847) and Wincenty Dunin-Marcinkiewicz (1807–1884). Their writings and poetry followed the Romantic tradition and were addressed to the upper classes. The Realist tradition—which reached out to the peasants, that is, the majority of the Belarussian people—was established by nationalists Kastus Kalinowski (1838–1864) and Frantsyszek Boguszewicz (1840–1900). This tradition was continued by classical authors: poet Maksim Bogdanowicz (1891–1917), who is famous for the collection of sonnets *Vianok* (1913); Janka Kupala (1882–1942), a major figure in the national revival and author of what is usually considered the single most important piece of Belarussian literature, the tragicomedy *Tuteyshya* (1922; The locals); and poet Jakub Kolas (1882–1956), who wrote the epics *Novaya Ziamlia* (1923; New land) and *Symon Muzyka* (1925; Symon the musician). These writers worked at a time when the transition from writing Belarussian in the Latin script to using the Russian Cyrillic script was completed.

After the Russian Revolution (1917), a wave of Belarussian literature was produced under Communist censorship. Talented authors of the period included Ivan Melezh (1921–1976), who truthfully depicted controversies of the collectivization of the land; historical novelist Uladzimir Karatkevich (1930–1984); and Ales Adamovich (1927–1993) and Vasil Bykau (1924–2003), who both wrote about World War II (1939–1945) and its effects. At the same time, Belarussian emigrants established their own literature; notable representatives include poets Larysa Heniyush (1910–1983), who was forcefully returned to Belarus from Czechoslovakia and was sent to a Soviet Siberian prison camp, and Ryhor Krushina (1907–1979), who lived in New York. After President Alexander Lukashenko (born 1954; in office since 1994) came to power, the Belarussian Writers Association was forcibly dissolved because its members opposed his authoritarian regime.

ART AND ARCHITECTURE

There are few surviving examples of early architecture in Belarus because, prior to the seventeenth century, the main building

The National Library of Belarus in Minsk (opened in 2006) is the city's best-known modern building.

material was timber, and Belarus was at the crossroads of major military conflicts. The oldest architectural monuments are the eleventh-century Saint Sophia Cathedral in Polatsk and the Church of Saints Barys and Hleb in Hrodna, which were both originally built in the Byzantine style. Other important medieval landmarks include the thirteenth-century White Tower in Kamyanets, which features distinctive Baltic brickwork, and the ruins of the thirteenth-century Navahrudak Castle and the fourteenth-century Kreva Castle. While the castle of Mir (c. 1510) preserved its original Gothic style, the sixteenth-century castle of Niasvizh lost most of its original Renaissance style in renovations.

Polish rule and, with it, the promotion of Roman Catholicism brought the baroque style as exemplified by numerous seventeenth- and eighteenth-century Jesuit, Bernardine, Bridgettine, and Dominican churches and monasteries. Russian rule resulted in the rebuilding of old Gothic and baroque churches in the Byzantine style and in the construction of new churches in the Russian Revival style, which combined Russian and Byzantine traditions.

As most large cities suffered extensive damage in World War II, they were built anew in the monumental Soviet style of Socialist Realism. The Soviet era also survives in the 1950s and 1960s multistory apartment buildings, which were quickly and cheaply built from prefabricated concrete panels and contained hundreds of small accommodations. Post-Soviet architecture is represented by the high-rise diamond-shaped building of the National Library in Minsk, the national capital, as well as hockey arenas built all over the country by order of President Lukashenko.

The most popular traditional folk arts are straw weaving and embroidery of ceremonial linen towels known as *rushnik*. In the seventeenth century, a distinct school of Belarussian icon painting emerged, which fused the Eastern Byzantine iconographic tradition with the technical and stylistic methods of European Renaissance painting. Fine arts developed in Belarus only in the nineteenth century and are represented by the works of portraitists Józef Oleszkiewicz (1777–1830) and Walenty Walkowicz (1800–1842), landscape painter Napoleon Orda (1807–1883), and still-life artist Ivan Khrutsky (1810–1885). A significant school of fine arts was established in the late nineteenth century in Vitsyebsk by Saint Petersburg–trained artist Yehuda Pen (1854–1937), who led the way for what art critics call the Jewish Renaissance in Belarussian fine arts. His students included famous Belarussian-born artists who became French, such as Marc Chagall (1887–1985), Pinchus Kremegne (1890–1981), and Ossip Zadkine (1890–1967). In his post as commissar of arts for the Vitsyebsk Region, Chagall founded the Vitsyebsk Arts School in 1918. Another significant school of painting was established in Minsk by Paris-trained portraitist Jankel Kruger (1869–1940). Major Belarus-based artists include landscapist Vitaut Bialynitski-Birulia (1872–1957), landscape painter Jazep Drazdowicz (1888–1954), and sculptor Zair Azhur (1908–1995).

The sixteenth-century Mir Castle Complex is now a UNESCO World Heritage site.

MUSIC AND PERFORMING ARTS

Choral singing is at the heart of Belarussian musical tradition. The most popular folk instruments are various pipes, the tambourine, the hurdy-gurdy, the fiddle, and, above all, the dulcimer. The earliest evidence of distinctive ecclesiastical music is documented in the liturgical manuscripts of Bohdan Anisimowicz (flourished 1598–1601). Western-style music arrived in the region in the eighteenth century with French and Italian artists who directed orchestras and opera companies of serfs in the courts of wealthy nobles, notably Radziwill princes in Niasvizh and the Oginski princes in Slonim.

The first significant classical composers in what is now Belarus were the painter Napoleon Orda and Stanislaw Moniuszko (1819–1972). The latter is famous for the opera *Sialianka* (1852) and for establishing the Polish national opera. The Belarussian National Music Academy, the Philharmonic Society, and the national opera and ballet companies were founded in the 1930s and were significantly influenced by the Russian musical tradition. The most notable Soviet-era composers were Yauhen Tsikotsky (1893–1970), composer of the operas *Mikhas Padhorny* (1939) and *Alesya* (1944), and Yauhen Hlebau (1929–2000), famous for the opera *Tvaya Viasna* (1963; Your spring) and the ballet *Alpiyskaya Balada* (1967; Alpine ballad). The leading Belarussian composer is Dmitry Smolsky (born 1937), whose most successful works include his first piano concerto (1960), the symphonic poem *Belarus* (1960), and his second dulcimer concerto (1974).

U.S. composer Irving Berlin (Israel Isidore Baline; 1888–1989) was born in Belarus, but little of his music reached Belarussians in his lifetime. During the Soviet era, the authorities did not allow much Western music and instead promoted local music. In the 1970 and 1980s, Belarussian bands such as Siabry, Pesniary, and Verasy became popular across the Soviet Union. They combined folk music with as much rock music as they dared. From the 1980s, Western music was no longer restricted, and a new generation of Belarussian rock bands emerged. In modern times, President Lukashenko promotes local music and decreed that both state and independent media devote at least 75 percent of their music broadcast to local artists. However, the state promotes only musicians who conform to state ideology. Rock bands may only perform at non-state-owned venues and sell their records through private retailers.

FESTIVALS AND CEREMONIES

The nation stages a number of modern popular annual music festivals such as the international festival of classical music, Minsk Spring (established 1980), and the state-sponsored festival of pop music, Slavic Bazaar, held in Vitsyebsk since 1992.

Some traditional festivals date from pre-Christian times. They include Kupalle, the summer solstice celebration involving dancing in circles around a bonfire, wearing flower garlands, and searching for the *paparats* flower, which was believed to have magical properties. Dazhynki, which celebrates the harvest in September with decorated wheat sheaves, singing, and dancing, has in modern times acquired elements of state propaganda, including a Soviet-style parade of agricultural machinery and honors for the winners of a national harvesting competition. Forefathers' Eve (October 31–November 1) precedes All Saints' and All Souls' celebrations by commemorating the deceased,

taking care of graveyards, and leaving food and drink for the dead.

Public holidays begin with secular New Year's Day (January 1) and are followed by Russian Orthodox Christmas (January 7). Women's Day (March 8) has been celebrated since the Soviet era. Russian Orthodox Easter usually falls in April and is celebrated by the Orthodox community; Catholic Easter, which may precede it, is also a public holiday. Constitution Day (March 15) marks the adoption of the constitution in 1994. Labor Day (May 1) is another surviving Soviet tradition that was originally established to celebrate the unity of workers. Victory Day (May 9) commemorates the capitulation of Nazi Germany at the end of World War II.

National Day is Independence Day (July 3), which is actually the anniversary of the liberation of Minsk in 1944. The date of modern independence was August 25, 1991, which is not celebrated. Before President Lukashenko came to power, Independence Day was celebrated on March 25, the anniversary of the declaration of the anti-Communist republic in 1918. Today, this is marked by rallies of the political opposition as Freedom Day, and opposition activists are routinely arrested at these events. Other public holidays include April 2 (Unity of the Peoples of Belarus and Russia Day), Forefathers' Eve, November 7 (the anniversary of the 1917 Bolshevik coup in Russia), Roman Catholic Christmas Day (December 25), and Orthodox Christmas Day (January 7).

FOOD AND DRINK

Belarussian cuisine is typically hearty and simple. The staple foods are potato, cereals, and meats. There are said to be more than 300 Belarussian potato dishes, including *draniki* (potato pancakes), *kalduny* (stuffed potato dumplings), and *babka* (potato and pork pie). Both rye and wheat are used to make bread, and *kasha* is a porridge made of oats, barley, or buckwheat. Traditional meat dishes include *kumpiak* (cured ham), *kalbasa* (pork sausage), *saltsison* (pork intestines boiled in the animal's stomach), *sala* (nonrendered pork fat cured with salt and herbs), and Lithuanian *bigos* (beef cooked with sauerkraut). Celebratory meals may include game such as wild boar, deer, elk (moose), duck, partridge, and fish such as perch, pike, carp, and eel. Stuffed carp in aspic is a popular Christmas dish adopted from Jewish cuisine. Traditional dairy dishes include sweet or sour milk, *smiatana* (sour cream), and a variety of soft cheeses. Vegetables enjoyed as starters include gherkins. Pickles (of tomatoes, peppers, and garlic) are commonly served, and side dishes include salads, sauerkraut, and Russian *salianka* (a mix of sauerkraut, onions, cucumbers, tomatoes, and wild mushrooms).

Traditional soft drinks are made of cranberries, blackberries, and other wild berries by diluting juice with water or by boiling them with a pinch of starch to create a thick drink called *kisel*. Another traditional drink is *kvass*, a slightly alcoholic drink made from rye bread. Beer and vodka are the favorite alcoholic drinks. In rural areas, people still distill their own alcohol from fermented potatoes or beets, known as *harelka*, even though it is illegal. The popularity of wine is growing but it is limited because it is imported and expensive.

P. OVSEIKO, A. KHARYTANOVICH

The Island of Tears monument in Minsk was constructed in the memory of the soldiers who died in the Russian conflict with Afghanistan (1979–1988).

DAILY LIFE

Society in Belarus has been profoundly influenced by two centuries of Russian rule from the late eighteenth century and seven decades of Communism until 1991. Foreign rule and authoritarianism shaped how people live in a society that, even in modern times, is still under authoritarian rule.

Modern Belarus is relatively homogenous, although there is also a strong Russian presence. Europeans account for virtually 100 percent of the population, and Belarus is a nation that has experienced little modern immigration, except for a minority of Armenians, Georgians, and Azeris who have come to Belarus to seek better employment prospects than in their Caucasian homelands. In modern times, some 81 percent of the population of Belarus are Belarussians (also given as Belarusians), while Russians account for 11 percent, Poles 4 percent, Ukrainians 2 percent, and others (mainly from within the former Soviet Union) 2 percent. Since independence in 1991, the size of the ethnic minorities has declined.

RELIGION

Religion was persecuted until the 1980s under the former Soviet Union and, as a result, religious practice became uncommon. Now, some 40–45 percent of the population are described as Russian Orthodox, although only about 8 percent or fewer are practicing. An unknown percentage are members of the persecuted Belarussian Autocephalous Orthodox Church. Roman Catholics account for 10 percent of the population, although only 5 percent or fewer are practicing. Other Christians include the Belarussian Greek Catholic Church, representing 1 percent of the population, and Baptists, Seventh-Day Adventists, Evangelical Christians, Old Believers, Lutherans, and other Christians, who together account for 2 percent. Jews, Sunni Muslims, and others account for another 1 percent, while more than 35 percent of Belarussians are nonreligious.

For the last six hundred years, the Roman Catholic Church and the Russian Orthodox Church have competed for the allegiance of Belarussian Christians. Today, the Russian Orthodox Church enjoys the support of the authoritarian regime of President Alexander Lukashenko (born 1954; in office from 1994) and other religions are actively discriminated against or even suppressed.

In the late tenth century, Greek missionaries brought Christianity to the Belarussian lands. However, in the late fourteenth century, the ruler of Lithuania (of which Belarus was part) converted to Roman Catholicism in order to gain the Polish throne. This conversion prompted the spread of Catholicism in the region and the establishment of the Greek Catholic Church

(in 1595), which entered full communion with Rome while keeping the (former Orthodox) Byzantine rite. After the Belarussian lands were annexed by the Russian Empire in the late eighteenth century (when Poland was partitioned by its neighbors), the authorities suppressed the Greek Catholic Church in favor of the Russian Orthodox Church. During the Soviet era (from 1919), the Russian Orthodox Church cooperated with the Communists in order to survive, and, since independence, it has enjoyed state support.

Catholicism flourished after the fall of Communism, but since President Lukashenko came to power in 1994, the Catholic Church has been discriminated against by the state. It is perceived by the authorities as a threat to the state-sponsored Orthodox Church. In 1989–1990, the Russian Orthodox Church in Belarus was given a separate identity when the Belarussian Orthodox Church, an exarchate (semiautonomous branch) of the Russian Church was created. However, the church remains under effective Russian control; its head is Russian, and Russian is the principal language of its worship. The Belarussian

Housing

Industrialization and rapid urbanization started in Belarus only in the 1920s during the Soviet era, but was halted by war. Before the Nazi invasion, the population of Belarus was 9.2 million people. After the liberation (1944), it was only 6.3 million; out of 270 towns, 209 were virtually destroyed, and some five thousand villages were devastated during the occupation. After 1945, with investment from the rest of the Soviet Union, Belarus's infrastructure was rebuilt. In 1940, 21 percent of the population lived in towns and, in 1959, 31 percent; in modern times, 73 percent of the population of Belarus are urban. Because of the pressure of urbanization and the postwar necessity to rebuild housing, most urban housing stock consists of multistory apartment buildings assembled from prefabricated concrete panels or built quickly from bricks. Rural dwellers live in individual homes of higher quality. Because the majority of the urban population, or their parents, were born outside the cities, it is relatively common among urban people to have rural homes (dachas) where they spend weekends and grow fruits and vegetables for their own consumption.

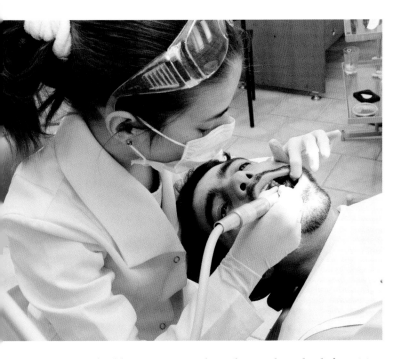

State health care exists in Belarus, but at a lower level of provision than in the Soviet era.

Orthodox Autocephalous Church, an officially unrecognized branch of Orthodoxy that refused to compromise with the Soviet authorities, experiences persecution. This church has a presence in the emigré Belarussian population. The Greek Catholic Church is also restricted.

In 2002, Belarus introduced legislation that proclaimed Russian Orthodoxy as the leading religion and recognized Catholicism, Judaism, Islam, and Evangelical Lutheranism as the only other legitimate religions. Despite the protests of the United Nations Commission on Human Rights in 2005, other religions are deemed illegal, and their activities are restricted. To date, the state has demolished a place of worship of the Belarussian Autocephalous Orthodox Church; it has persecuted Baptists, Jehovah Witnesses, and Adventist Protestants; and it has denied visas to and deported Polish Catholic priests.

In 1897, the Jewish population formed 14 percent of the population of the Belarussian lands. However, many Belarussian Jews migrated before or soon after the Russian Revolution (1917) because of poor economic conditions. Hundreds of thousands were murdered during the Holocaust in World War II (1939–1945), and tens of thousands emigrated during or after Soviet rule. Today, there are 50,000 Jews in Belarus. They have managed to recover only 9 out of 92 historic synagogues and to reestablish a number of religious schools.

Islam was brought to the area that is now Belarus in the fourteenth century, when Tatars from Crimea and farther east were invited to settle in Lithuania to guard its borders against Muscovy. Today, the Muslim population of Belarus includes a 10,000-strong Tatar community as well as thousands of Muslim immigrants from the former Soviet Union. There are four mosques in the country.

FAMILY AND SOCIETY

Family structure and the nature of society in Belarus are undergoing profound changes and are subject to a clash of values of three generations. While grandparents were brought up in a patriarchal family typical of agrarian society, the generation of parents experienced an urbanized industrial society. Their children, in turn, are influenced by the advent of postindustrial society. Social values are also influenced by the authoritarian government, which intervenes in daily life to a greater degree than the governments of Western countries.

On average, Belarussian men and women marry in their early twenties, but 70 percent of marriages end in divorce. Early marriages are driven by cultural tradition, a desire to escape the parental home, and state-sponsored loans for newlyweds to buy or build housing. Despite state polices to encourage a high birthrate, the total fertility rate has declined to 1.2 children per woman (2007), and even though Belarus has a slightly positive net migration, the population of the country has steadily decreased since the fall of Communism. During the Soviet era, equal employment opportunities were achieved for women, and unjustifiable absence from work was an offense. This heritage, along with the heavy intervention of the state in the economy, accounts for the fact that almost as many women are in full-time employment as men.

HEALTH AND WELFARE

A comprehensive health care service was established in Belarus in the Soviet era. A reduced version of this system still exists and is funded by taxation. State health care was successful in alleviating high morbidity and mortality associated with infectious diseases, and, by the end of the 1960s, life expectancy at birth in Belarus was comparable to that in the United States. However, from the 1970s, the Belarussian health care system has failed to effectively tackle cardiovascular diseases and cancers, which today are the most common causes of death. This failure is mainly due to the reluctance of the population to give up a calorie- and fat-rich diet, smoking, and drinking, coupled with a lack of hard currency needed to purchase modern Western medical technology and drugs. Moreover, since 1986, Belarus has experienced the devastating impact of the Chernobyl disaster: 70 percent of the radioactive fallout from the accident at the nuclear facility at Chernobyl, in neighboring Ukraine, fell in Belarus. As a result, Belarussians have experienced a high level of cancers.

Since the dissolution of the Soviet Union, public health funding has slowly increased, but, in terms of the utilization of modern drugs and medical technology, Belarussian health care lags behind affluent western European countries. Today, hospitals and clinics are often crowded, and patients customarily give illicit payments to doctors in order to move up waiting lists. In 2007, the average life expectancy in Belarus was 64.6 years for men and 76.4 years for women, which is slightly lower than the life expectancy in 1990.

METROPOLITAN AREAS, 2006 POPULATION

Urban population	78 percent
Moscow	12,400,000
Moscow City	10,425,000
Saint Petersburg	4,581,000
Nizhny Novgorod	1,680,000
Nizhny Novgorod City	1,284,000
Novosibirsk	1,397,000
Samara	1,330,000
Samara City	1,143,000
Yekaterinburg	1,308,000
Volgograd	1,300,000
Volgograd City	992,000
Rostov-na-Donu	1,190,000
Rostov-na-Donu City	1,055,000
Chelyabinsk	1,230,000
Chelyabinsk City	1,093,000
Omsk	1,139,000
Kazan	1,113,000
Ufa	1,030,000
Perm	993,000
Krasnoyarsk	921,000
Voronezh	870,000
Voronezh City	846,000
Saratov	850,000
Krasnodar	710,000
Tol'yatti	705,000
Barnaul	675,000
Barnaul City	604,000
Ulyanovsk	617,000
Izhevsk	619,000
Yaroslavl	604,000
Vladivostok	584,000
Irkutsk	578,000
Khabarovsk	578,000
Novokuznetsk	562,000
Tyumen	542,000
Orenburg	534,000
Kemerovo	520,000
Ryazan	513,000
Penza	510,000
Tula	509,000
Naberezhnye-Chelny	507,000
Lipetsk	503,000
Astrakhan	499,000
Tomsk	490,000
Vyatka	468,000
Makhachkala	466,000
Cheboksary	442,000
Kaliningrad	424,000
Bryansk	420,000
Ivanovo	413,000
Magnitogorsk	413,000
Tver	406,000
Kursk	405,000

Source: Russian census authority estimates, 2006

NEIGHBORS AND LENGTH OF BORDERS*

Azerbaijan	177 miles (284 km)
Belarus	596 miles (959 km)
China	2,265 miles (3,645 km)
Estonia	180 miles (290 km)
Finland	816 miles (1,313 km)
Georgia*	449 miles (723 km)
Kazakhstan	4,255 miles (6,846 km)
North Korea	11 miles (18 km)
Latvia	181 miles (292 km)
Lithuania	141 miles (227 km)
Mongolia	2,139 miles (3,441 km)
Norway	122 miles (196 km)
Poland	268 miles (432 km)
Ukraine	979 miles (1,576 km)

* includes borders with the breakaway, but internationally unrecognized, republics of Abkhazia and South Ossetia

POPULATION

Population	142,754,000 (2006 government estimate)
Population density	22 per sq. mile (8 per sq. km)
Population growth	-0.5 percent a year
Birthrate	11.0 births per 1,000 of the population
Death rate	16.1 deaths per 1,000 of the population
Population under age 15	14.6 percent
Population over age 65	14.1 percent
Sex ratio	106 males for 100 females
Fertility rate	1.4 children per woman
Infant mortality rate	10.8 deaths per 1,000 live births
Life expectancy at birth	
Total population	65.9 years
Female	73.1 years
Male	59.2 years

FLAG

The flag of the Russian Federation is that of pre-revolutionary (pre-1917) Russia: three horizontal bands, from the top, white, blue, and red. The flag, which was readopted in 1991, originated under Peter I (the Great; 1672–1725).

NORWAY

Murmansk

MURMANSK

Barents
Sea

ARKHANGEL'SK

Novaya
Zemlya

Kara
Sea

FINLAND

SAINT
PETERSBURG
CITY

KALININGRAD

Kaliningrad

ESTONIA

POLAND

LATVIA

LITHUANIA

Saint
Petersburg

Pskov

LENINGRAD

Petrozavodsk

KARELIA
REPUBLIC

Arkhangel'sk

NENETS AUTONOMOUS PROVINCE

Nar'yan-Mar

BELARUS

PSKOV

Novgorod

NOVGOROD

Cherepovets

Syktyvkar

KOMI
REPUBLIC

Salekhard

YAMAL-NENETS
AUTONOMOUS PROVINCE

Yenisey

TVER

Tver

Vologda

Smolensk

Zelenograd

Yaroslavl

Kostroma

Ob

RUSSIA

UKRAINE

Bryansk

Kaluga

Moscow

⑧⑦

Ivanovo

Vladimir

Nizhny
Novgorod

Vyatka

KIROV

PERM
TERRITORY

Perm

KHANTY-MANSIY
AUTONOMOUS PROVINCE

Khanty-Mansiysk

Tula

Kursk

Orel

Ryazan

Dzerzhinsk

Yoshkar-Ola

⑤

Surgut

Ob

Lipetsk

Tambov

Cheboksary

⑥

Saransk

①

Kazan

Izhevsk

⑩

Naberezhnye-Chelny

Nizhny Tagil

KRASNOYARS
TERRITORY

Belgorod

Voronezh

Penza

PENZA

TATARSTAN

Ulyanovsk

Tol'yatti

REPUBLIC

SVERDLOVSK

Yekaterinburg

Black
Sea

Taganrog

ROSTOV

Shakhty

Rostov-
na-Donu

Saratov

Volga

Samara

BASHKORTOSTAN

Ufa

REPUBLIC

Sterlitamak

Chelyabinsk

Tyumen

TYUMEN

Kurgan

KURGAN

TOMSK

KRASNODAR
TERRITORY

ADYGEA
REPUBLIC

Maykop

Sochi

Volgograd

Volzhskij

Krasnodar

Stavropol

Elista

KALMYKIA
REPUBLIC

⑨

Orenburg

Magnitogorsk

Orsk

OMSK

Omsk

NOVOSIBIRSK

Tomsk

Cherkessk

Astrakhan

NORTH OSSETIA
REPUBLIC

③

②

Nalchik

Magas

Vladikavkaz

Groznyy

GEORGIA

INGUSHETIYA REPUBLIC

CHECHNYA REPUBLIC

Makhachkala

DAGESTAN
REPUBLIC

Caspian Sea

AZERBAIJAN

KAZAKHSTAN

Novosibirsk

Kemerovo

Krasnoyarsk

Novokuznetsk

Barnaul

ALTAY TERRITORY

④

Abakan

Gorno-Altaysk

Kyzyl

GORNO-ALTAY
REPUBLIC

TUVA REPUBLIC

MONGOLIA

| 0 | 100 | 400 miles |
| 0 | 160 | 640 km |

★ National capital

★ Regional, provincial, republic, and territorial capital

● Other city

— National border

— Regional, provincial, republic, and territorial border

Note: Administrative areas are classed as regions unless specified.
Any unnamed regions are named by their capitals.

ADMINISTRATIVE DIVISIONS (REGIONS UNLESS SPECIFIED)

① CHUVASH REPUBLIC

② KABARDINO-BALKARIA REPUBLIC

③ KARACHAY-CHERKESSIA REPUBLIC

④ KHAKASSIA REPUBLIC

⑤ MARIY-EL REPUBLIC

⑥ MORDOVIA REPUBLIC

⑦ MOSCOW

⑧ MOSCOW CITY

⑨ STAVROPOL TERRITORY

⑩ UDMURTIA REPUBLIC

★ National capital

★ Regional, provincial, republic, and territorial capital

● Other city

━ National border

─ Regional, provincial, republic, and territorial border

Note: Administrative areas are classed as regions unless specified.
Any unnamed regions are named by their capitals.

U.S.A.

ARCTIC OCEAN

Wrangel
Island

Chukchi
Sea

Bering Strait

East
Siberian
Sea

New
Siberian
Islands

Laptev
Sea

Anadyr'★

CHUKOT AUTONOMOUS
PROVINCE

Bering
Sea

KRASNOYARSK
TERRITORY

Lena

SAKHA
REPUBLIC

MAGADAN

R U S S I A

Siberia

Lena

Yakutsk★

Magadan ★

KAMCHATKA
TERRITORY

Sea of
Okhotsk

Petropavlovsk-
Kamchatskiy ★

Bratsk ●

IRKUTSK

BURYATIA
REPUBLIC

Lake
Baikal

ZABAYKALSKY
TERRITORY

AMUR

KHABAROVSK
TERRITORY

SAKHALIN

Komsomolsk-
na-Amure ●

Angarsk ● ● Irkutsk
● Ulan-Ude   ★ Chita

Blagoveshchensk ●

Khabarovsk ★

Yuzhno-
Sakhalinsk ★

Birobidzhan ★

YEVREY
AUTONOMOUS
REGION

J A P A N

MONGOLIA

CHINA

PRIMOR'YE
TERRITORY

★ Vladivostok

PACIFIC
OCEAN

NORTH
KOREA

0   100   400 miles

0   160   640 km

1357

ECONOMY

Currency	Russian ruble (RUB)
Exchange rate (2008)	$1 = RUB 27.52
Gross domestic product (2007)	$2.09 trillion
GDP per capita (2007)	$14,800
Unemployment rate (2007)	6.2 percent
Population under poverty line (2007)	15.8 percent
Exports	$355.5 billion (2007 CIA estimate)
Imports	$223.4 billion (2007 CIA estimate)

GOVERNMENT

Official country name	Russian Federation
Conventional short form	Russia
Former names	Soviet Union, Russian Soviet Federative Socialist Republic
Nationality	
noun	Russian
adjective	Russian
Official language	Russian
Capital city	Moscow
Type of government	Federal republic; limited democracy
Voting rights	18 years, universal
National anthem	"Gimn Rossiyskoy Federatsii" (Hymn of the Russian Federation)
National day	Russia Day, June 12 (1990; the anniversary of the declaration of sovereignty by the legislature of the Russian Soviet Federative Socialist Republic)

TRANSPORTATION

Railroads	66,584 miles (107,157 km), including 18,641 miles (30,000 km) of industrial and mining lines
Highways	579,863 miles (933,000 km)
Expressways	18,641 miles (30,000 km)
Other paved roads	450,484 miles (724,984 km)
Unpaved roads	110,614 miles (178,016 km)
Navigable waterways	63,380 miles (102,000 km)
Airports	
International airports	15
Paved runways	601

POPULATION PROFILE, 2007 ESTIMATES

Ethnic groups	
Europeans/Caucasian peoples	89 percent (of which Russians form 80 percent; Ukrainians 2 percent; Chechens 1 percent; Armenians, Belarussians, Germans, Ossetians, Moldovans, and other Europeans 2 percent; other Caucasian peoples 2 percent)
Turkic peoples	8 percent (including Tatars 4 percent; Bashkirs 1 percent; Chuvashs 1 percent; Kazakhs, Azeris, Yakuts, and others 2 percent)
Buryats, Mongols, Koreans, Kalmyks, and others	3 percent
Religions	
Russian Orthodox	16 percent; 70 percent identify with the Russian Orthodox culture
Sunni Islam	10–15 percent
Other Christians (Evangelicals, Baptists, Roman Catholics, Old Believers, and others)	2 percent
Nonreligious	65–70 percent
Languages	
Russian	83 percent as a first language, but almost universally understood
Tatar	3 percent
Ukrainian	2 percent
Bashkir	1 percent
Chechen	1 percent
Chuvash	1 percent
Others	9 percent
Adult literacy	over 99 percent

The port city of Vladivostok, on Russia's eastern coast.

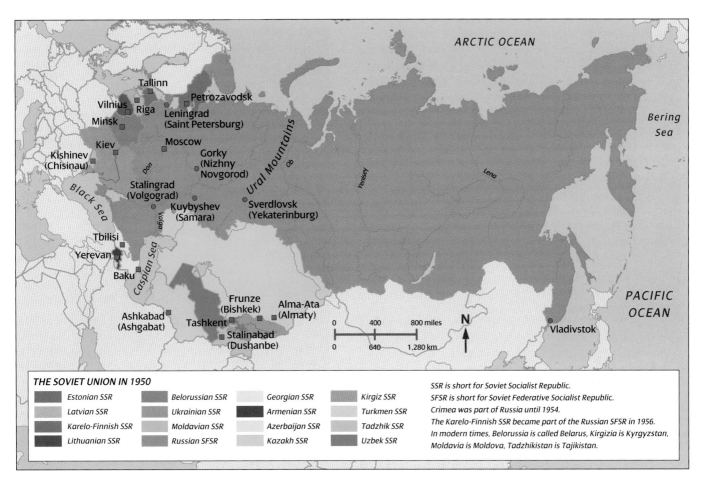

THE SOVIET UNION IN 1950

Estonian SSR	Belorussian SSR	Georgian SSR
Latvian SSR	Ukrainian SSR	Armenian SSR
Karelo-Finnish SSR	Moldavian SSR	Azerbaijan SSR
Lithuanian SSR	Russian SFSR	Kazakh SSR

Kirgiz SSR	Turkmen SSR
	Tadzhik SSR
	Uzbek SSR

SSR is short for Soviet Socialist Republic.
SFSR is short for Soviet Federative Socialist Republic.
Crimea was part of Russia until 1954.
The Karelo-Finnish SSR became part of the Russian SFSR in 1956.
In modern times, Belorussia is called Belarus, Kirgizia is Kyrgyzstan,
Moldavia is Moldova, Tadzhikistan is Tajikistan.

increased to 5 million soldiers. A number of measures for improvement of the organization and combat training of armies were instituted, but the efficiency of the forces had been compromised by the great number of officers, including military leaders, who had been executed during Stalin's purges.

In the Spanish Civil War (1936–1939), the Soviet Union aided the Republicans in their struggle against the conservative Nationalist forces. In November 1939, the Soviet Union invaded Finland, beginning the Soviet-Finnish Winter War (1939–1940). Soviet armies eventually defeated Finnish resistance, but the cost of this victory was considerable: 50,000 Red Army soldiers and officers were killed and 150,000 wounded. At the peace, Finland was obliged to cede its southeastern region to the Soviet Union.

In early 1939, the Soviet government agreed to consider an alliance with Great Britain and France in event of war with Germany. However, the (covert) Molotov-Ribbentrop Nazi-Soviet pact of August 1939 implicitly allowed Germany to invade Poland, while assigning Estonia, Latvia, and Lithuania, along with eastern Poland, to the Soviet Union. As a result, Soviet forces occupied eastern Poland and made military and other demands on Estonia, Latvia, and Lithuania, dictating a change of government and the establishment of military bases and "assistance" treaties. With puppet regimes installed in all three Baltic states, invasion by the Red Army ensured the "request" of Estonia, Latvia, and Lithuania to be incorporated in the Soviet Union. The Nazi-Soviet pact involved extensive economic and military cooperation between Germany and the Soviet Union and assumed nonaggression.

WORLD WAR II

Despite the pact, on June 22, 1941, German forces suddenly attacked the Soviet Union and began a full-scale offensive. Within a few days, much of the Soviet air force had been destroyed on the ground, while German tanks advanced deep into Soviet territory. Many tens of thousands of Soviet soldiers and officers were captured by the Germans, who advanced as far as Moscow, forcing the Soviet authorities to relocate, although the city did not fall.

Leningrad (since 1991 renamed Saint Petersburg) was a prime target for German forces, and the city was besieged for 900 days from September 1941 through January 1944. German forces besieged the city to the south and west and Finnish troops to the east—Finland fought the War of Continuation (1941–1944) in an attempt to regain territory lost to the Soviet Union in 1940. Up to 650,000 people died in Leningrad during the siege.

From 1941 through 1943, the Soviet authorities reorganized the economy (moving strategic installations to the Urals and beyond, out of reach of the German army) and also reformed the Soviet armed forces. Until early 1943, the Red Army was in retreat, but the Battle of Moscow began to turn the tide. Two battles were decisive in reversing the German advance. The battle of Stalingrad (now Volgograd) was one of the fiercest battles of World War II, which in the Soviet Union was called the Great Patriotic War. From mid-1942 through February 1943, a battle was fought for control of the city, the greater part of which was destroyed. However, German forces were cut off and obliged to surrender. In a major series of battles at Kursk (July–August 1943), the Soviets lost more than half a million personnel, but they inflicted a defeat on the Germans, giving the Soviets the initiative to take the offensive.

In March 1944, the Red Army crossed the western boundary of the Soviet Union and, in April 1945, Russian units met American troops along the Elbe River in central Germany. On May 2, Berlin, the German national capital, fell to the Red Army, and, on May 8, Germany surrendered unconditionally.

AFTER THE WAR

For the Soviet Union, the war brought tremendous human losses and material destruction. The total number of Soviet military and civilian dead remains uncertain, but modern historians suggest a figure of 27 million people. Material losses were enormous: during the war, both armies had employed a scorched-earth policy, trying to destroy all that could be of military value to the enemy. As a result, the economy of the Soviet Union was ruined.

On the other hand, the war led to a strong surge of patriotism and nationalism, and the army acquired new prominence and prestige. Feeling more secure, the Soviet authorities relaxed their persecution of the Orthodox Church, and the general level of repression was eased. The war had also made the Soviet Union a world power, and the nation had increased its territory, adding Estonia, Latvia, Lithuania, Moldavia (now Moldova) and Finno-Karelia as Union republics and annexing eastern Poland to Belorussia (modern Belarus). At the same time, with the Soviet Red Army in much of central and eastern Europe, which it had liberated, a series of Communist satellite states were established in Poland, Czechoslovakia, Romania, Hungary, Albania, and Bulgaria. As a result, the Soviet Union came to dominate eastern Europe.

After the war, the Soviet people had to rebuild the economy. Stalin introduced new five-year plans and continued the nation's industrial and economic advance. The Fourth Five-Year Plan gained a boost from reparations and other payments from defeated Germany and its allies. Industrial production dramatically grew, and agricultural production increased, although agriculture remained a major weakness of the Soviet economy.

Union-wide elections were held in 1946 for the first time since 1937. Republican and other local elections also took place. However, Soviet power continued to attempt to shape society, aiming to produce citizens who complied with the demands of the state. Repression recommenced, and labor camps in the GULAG were filled with citizens of the newly added republics—large numbers of Estonians, Latvians, and Lithuanians were sent to Siberia. Also, victorious Soviet soldiers and officers from the

Undated portrait of Joseph Stalin (1879–1953; leader of the Soviet Communist Party and effectively ruler of the Soviet Union 1922–1953).

recent war, intellectuals, Jews, and others found themselves as political exiles in the labor camps. Science, literature, and the arts all suffered from the imposition of censorship. At the same time, Stalin introduced a stifling personality cult.

As Soviet power expanded into eastern and central Europe, the wartime cooperation between the Soviet Union and its Western allies broke down. The world polarized into Communist and anti-Communist blocks, headed by the Soviet Union and the United States, respectively. The Cold War, the period of rivalry between these two blocks, began, often fought in proxy wars in developing countries and made more tense by the acquisition of nuclear weapons by the Soviet Union. Stalin had transformed the Soviet Union into a command economy, a dictatorship run by himself rather than the Communist Party apparatus, with compliance enforced by the NKVD. Some ethnic minorities were forcibly resettled; for example, the Crimean Tatars were moved to Central Asia, being accused of collaborating with the Germans. Soviet society was repressed, and many looked for new freedoms when the dictator died in office in March 1953.

S. KYULLENEN

The Soviet Union under Khrushchev and Brezhnev

After the death of Joseph Stalin (1879–1953), Nikita Khrushchev (1894–1971; in office as general secretary of the Communist Party 1953–1964) came to power, followed by Leonid Brezhnev (1906–1982; in office 1964–1982). Under these leaders, the Soviet Union continued a period of rivalry (the Cold War) with the United States, although there were also times of rapprochement.

A short struggle for power, won by Khrushchev, followed the death in office of Soviet dictator Joseph Stalin. Then, a new period in Soviet history began, often referred to as *ottepel* (literally, "the thaw").

KHRUSHCHEV

A clear break with the Stalinist past came in a closed session of the Twentieth Communist Party Congress in February 1956, when Khrushchev made a speech, condemning the cult of personality of Stalin, repression under the late dictator, and other "mistakes." As a result, many political prisoners were released from the GULAG, the network of labor camps across Siberia, and were rehabilitated. Censorship was relaxed, though not abolished, and Soviet citizens came to enjoy more (though strictly limited) freedom.

Khrushchev directed the attention of the Soviet government toward social and economical problems. He prioritized agriculture and improved the conditions of those living and working on state farms and collectives. Previously, the overwhelming majority of agricultural workers, former peasants, were effectively tied to their farms and had no internal passports, which were necessary for them to be able to live somewhere else. People within the Soviet Union could not live where they wished but had to register their residence, producing an internal passport. People who came from outside a large city did not have the right of permanent residence in the city and obtained "limited rights" status through employment and were expected to return to their original homes when the period of employment ended. Khrushchev gave internal passports to rural workers, allowing them to move out of poor villages to the major cities.

FOREIGN RELATIONS

The Khrushchev era was also remarkable for its technological achievements. New types of weapons were created; space research developed and, in April 1961, the Soviet Union launched the first manned space satellite. Foreign policy of the Soviet Union under Khrushchev was also liberalized. Khrushchev's "thaw" was highlighted internationally by his 1954 visit to Beijing, China, and 1955 visit to Belgrade, Yugoslavia, reestablishing more cordial relations with Communist countries with which ties had been strained. Diplomacy continued with Khrushchev's 1955 meeting with U.S. president Dwight Eisenhower (1890–1969; in office 1953–1961) and culminated with Khrushchev's 1959 visit to the United States. In 1954–1956, the Soviet Union conducted separate negotiations that reestablished the independence of Austria, opened diplomatic relations with West Germany, and brought a peace treaty with Japan.

However, Khrushchev's reforms were not well-prepared. Much policy was either based on ideology or was rooted in his spontaneous, emotional character. Thus, in 1962, the Soviet government decided to base missiles in Cuba. Tension between the Soviet Union and the United States during the Cuban missile crisis at one time appeared to be leading toward war. Eventually, a compromise was reached and the Soviets backed down. Under Khrushchev, the Soviet Red Army also invaded Hungary to suppress a popular anti-Communist uprising in 1956.

The Soviet centralized command system of administration could not change in essence and remained totalitarian. The authorities promised the construction of a prosperous Communist society in the near future, but Khrushchev's government made economic errors, compromising the existing, meager prosperity. Consequently, opposition to Khrushchev in the Communist Party became stronger and, in October 1964, he was removed from power. The office of general secretary of the

A titanium monument to Yuri Gagarin (1934–1982)—the first man in space—was erected in 1980 in Moscow.

Communist Party was assumed by Leonid Brezhnev (1906–1982; in office 1964–1982) and the office of prime minister, which had also been held by Khrushchev since 1958, by Aleksey Kosygin (1904–1980; in office 1964–1980).

BREZHNEV

The period from 1964 through 1982 is often called the Years of Stagnation. Kosygin attempted to implement economic reforms to shift the economic emphasis from heavy industry and military production toward light industry and the production of consumer goods. Brezhnev did not support this policy and blocked Kosygin's reforms. Instead, Brezhnev undid many of the reforms of the Khrushchev era and followed some of the policies of Stalin.

Under Brezhnev, the Soviet economy prioritized industrial growth and the space program. Large resources were devoted to military expenditure. The Cold War gathered strength, and, despite Soviet statements of peace and collaboration, the Soviet government adopted an aggressive foreign policy. In the summer of 1968, the Soviet Army invaded Czechoslovakia, after a period known as the Prague Spring, when Czechoslovak Communist Party leader Alexander Dubcek (1921–1992; in office 1968–1969) attempted to liberalize the regime. Soviet forces ousted Dubcek and reinstated a hard-line dictatorship. In 1979, the Soviets

supported a coup in Afghanistan and sent troops into that country, where they eventually became bogged down in an unwinnable conflict. Under Brezhnev, the indirect military confrontation between the Soviet Union and the United States, as well as the arms race, continued.

Brezhnev's authority grew with the years, and a cult of personality also developed around the Soviet leader. Persecution of political dissidents increased, and widespread repression was directed against representatives of national minorities (who were becoming more resentful of Soviet rule), religious practitioners, and intellectuals. Some eminent people were exiled, either internally to Siberia or abroad. On the other hand, most Soviet people were not allowed to go abroad, and the number of foreigners coming to the Soviet Union, as well as the places that they were allowed to visit, were limited. Those Soviet citizens who were allowed abroad, such as athletes and artists, sometimes defected, such as famous ballet dancers Rudolf Nureyev (1938–1993) in 1961; Natalia Makarova (born 1940) in 1970; and Mikhail Baryshnikov (born 1948) in 1974.

The KGB (State Security Committee), the latest in a number of secret police authorities (founded in 1954), confined political dissidents in psychiatric wards and prisons. Propaganda proclaimed the economic and political successes of a socialist society, and no other viewpoint was heard. There were no independent channels of radio or television or other independent media. Brezhnev declared his time as the period of "developed socialism," but the economic progress that was made at the time owed more to a boom in oil prices in the 1970s than to any measures taken by the Soviet authorities.

Despite increased revenue from oil, the Soviet economy was in trouble, with agriculture and agriculture-related industry unable to feed the population. Although it had great agricultural resources, the Soviet Union had to import grain, paid for in U.S. dollars. The steep rise of oil prices in the mid-1970s brought slight improvements in the standard of living. However, improvements were not experienced by all. Corruption was evident. While the Soviet authorities promised universal welfare and a global victory of Communism, the most privileged officials enjoyed a much higher standard of living than that of ordinary citizens. The elite had access to travel, clothing, cars, books, and other products that most people could not obtain. In this environment, a covert society flourished. Filmmakers and writers made covert criticisms of the system in movies and plays; illegal publications (*samizdat*) of prohibited books circulated; and an unregistered gray economy provided some of the items that the Communist economy could not.

In the late 1970s and early 1980s, the Soviet economic situation deteriorated. A vast expenditure on defense and prestige projects left fewer resources for more basic concerns. The leadership seemed out of touch, with a gerontocracy (a group of elderly people holding the senior posts) in power. This group did not attempt reforms and opted for short-term solutions. When Brezhnev died in 1982, the Soviet system was beginning to collapse, although the true extent of its problems was not evident at the time.

S. KYULLENEN

The Last Years of the Soviet Union

After 1982, two short-lived leaders ruled Russia. They were followed by Mikhail Gorbachev (born 1931; in office as leader of the Communist Party 1985–1991 and as chief of state, later president, 1989–1991). Gorbachev inherited a system that proved incapable of reform and, in late 1991, the Soviet Union collapsed.

Most Soviet leaders stayed in power until death. After Leonid Brezhnev (1906–1982; in office 1964–1982), the nation was ruled by Yuri Andropov (1914–1984; in office as general secretary of the Communist Party 1982–1984 and as chief of state 1983–1984) and Konstantin Chernenko (1911–1985; similarly in office 1984–1985). Under these short-lived elderly leaders, the economic, social, and political problems of the Soviet Union became more evident, but neither was in office long enough to achieve anything substantial.

GORBACHEV

In 1985, Mikhail Gorbachev assumed office as general secretary of the Communist Party. He represented a new type of Soviet leader. He was (by Soviet standards) young, only 54 years old. He had endured a tough childhood under the totalitarian leadership of Joseph Stalin (1879–1953); from his early years, he knew about the poverty of agricultural workers, and he was well-educated, with degrees in economics and law. As a member of the Communist leadership, he had had opportunities to travel abroad; this would profoundly affect his political and social views. His foreign visits, leading Soviet delegations, took him to West Germany, Canada, and Great Britain, and the evident prosperity and modernity of these societies contrasted with a Soviet system that was in obvious need of reform.

Coming to power, Gorbachev faced severe economic and other problems. Owing to falling oil prices, state revenues (already overextended through large-scale expenditure on defense and the space program) were reduced. Food products were not sufficient to meet demand; labor productivity was falling, in part because of lack of incentives; and alcoholism affected much of the male workforce and placed a burden on the health care system. The centrally planned Soviet economy was on the verge of collapse.

At the same time, the Soviet Union faced a major environmental crisis, in April 1986, when an accident at the Chernobyl nuclear power facility, in northern Ukraine, led to the emission of radiation. The incident led to fatalities, the cordoning off of large areas in Belorussia (modern Belarus) owing to radioactive fallout, and a loss of credibility internationally by the Soviet leadership. The Soviet official reaction was perceived in Ukraine in particular as inadequate and increased discontent with Soviet rule in that republic.

PERESTROIKA AND GLASNOST

Gorbachev undertook reforms, which shocked not just the Soviet Union, but surprised the international community. He introduced the policy of perestroika (restructuring), under which he attempted to revive and restructure the economy in a new way: still socialist but with realistic prices, some element of profit and loss, and incentives. He did not wish to undermine the Soviet system, only to make it more efficient. Eventually, the task proved impossible.

Gorbachev initiated a campaign against the consumption of alcohol. The excessive consumption of vodka by Russian men, in particular, was creating health problems and reducing life expectancy and productivity at work. Gorbachev's policy of glasnost (openness) brought free expression and a relaxation of censorship. Literary censorship was relaxed, and many previously prohibited books were published. International movies were released in cinemas throughout the Soviet Union, and a stream of information about environmental pollution, the excesses of Stalin's dictatorship, the labor camps for political prisoners, and previous abuses of power became available.

At the same time, Gorbachev created a new supreme legislative body, the Congress of People's Deputies. This consisted of 2,250 members, elected under a complicated system. This body was charged with electing a new model Supreme Soviet of 450 members, to which short-term legislative powers were delegated. These were not Western-style institutions, but the reforms did admit the principle of dissent into official Soviet politics. Gorbachev was then elected to the new post of president of the Soviet Union in 1990.

Gorbachev brought unprecedented changes and liberalization to the Soviet Union. The Law on Cooperatives, enacted in May 1988, permitted private ownership of businesses in the service, manufacturing, and foreign-trade sectors. This measure overturned more than 60 years of state ownership of the economy. At the same time, many dissidents were allowed back from internal and external exile or were released from prison, and some non-Communists were encouraged to participate in public life.

FOREIGN AFFAIRS

In foreign affairs, Gorbachev pursued similar policies of reform. He became popular abroad because of his friendliness and accessibility, and he removed ideology from foreign and security policy making, arguing that all states were interdependent. The eastern European Communist countries were freed from the prospect of Soviet military intervention if they began their own reforms, which would inevitably change the Communist system. Subsequently, they all ousted their Communist governments and embraced democracy. Soviet troops were also recalled from Afghanistan, where they had proved ineffective against spirited Afghan resistance to their intervention.

Gorbachev held summits with U.S. president Ronald Reagan (1911–2004; in office 1981–1989), and he proposed the elimination of all nuclear weapons by the year 2000 and the establishment of a system of comprehensive security. He also met with U.S. president George Bush (born 1924; in office 1989–1993), and they signed two historic agreements: the Conventional Forces in Europe Treaty (1990) and the Strategic Arms Reduction Talks (START) treaty. With these agreements, the era of the Cold War (rivalry between the Soviet Union and the United States and its allies) and the arms race seemed to be over.

THE DISSOLUTION OF THE SOVIET UNION

The economic effects of perestroika were less successful than hoped. The old Soviet systems of tax collection and contributions and of central planning did not raise enough revenue for necessary economic reforms. The state debt was continuously growing. Numerous shortages provoked strikes in different parts of the country, and long lines for basic food items showed that the partial introduction of a market economy was not enough to help.

In the Soviet Union's 15 constituent republics, active independence movements could operate under glasnost. The Baltic states elected nationalist, non-Communist administrations and tried to secede. National movements gathered strength in the Caucasus, particular among Georgians and Armenians. At the

A Russian stamp from 1977, featuring Leonid Brezhnev (1906–1982; in office 1964–1982).

same time, discontent at the Soviet mishandling of the Chernobyl accident stirred increased separatism in Ukraine. Ethnic riots took place in parts of Central Asia, and there, as elsewhere when Soviet unity appeared threatened, the KGB tried to suppress popular unrest. However, the structure of the Soviet Union was coming apart, and the theoretical right of secession of the Union republics was about to become a reality. Lithuania had proclaimed independence in 1990, but this was not effective.

In this chaos, Gorbachev's popularity declined. Many political forces struggled for power, and Gorbachev and his supporters attempted to save the unity of the Soviet system and prepared a new Union Treaty. Some hard-line Communist leaders tried to stop this process of democratization, and, in August 1991, they made an unsuccessful attempt to take power in a coup, briefly detaining Gorbachev. As a result, Gorbachev's power and influence were greatly diminished.

New politicians appeared at that time, urging further reforms. Among them was Boris Yeltsin (1931–2007; in office as president of Russia 1991–1999), who became the first popularly elected president of the Russian Soviet Federative Socialist Republic (later the Russian Federation). In August 1991, Estonia and Latvia followed Lithuania's earlier example and declared the restoration of the independence they had lost half a century earlier. Their efforts were successful, and international recognition followed. By the fall, Ukraine, Belarus, Moldova, Georgia, Armenia, Azerbaijan, Kyrgyzstan, Uzbekistan, Tajikistan, and Turkmenistan declared their sovereignty. The presidents of Russia, Ukraine, and Belarus met on December 8 and declared the end of the Soviet Union. Gorbachev was presented with a fait accompli and had to agree with Yeltsin to dissolve the Soviet Union. Gorbachev resigned on December 25; two days later, on December 27, Yeltsin became chief of state of a newly independent Russia.

S. KYULLENEN

Modern Russia

Since the Russian Federation became an independent state in December 1991, the nation has adopted a free market but has experienced several economic crises. However, high oil and natural gas prices helped bring a recovery in the twenty-first century; at the same time, the state became more authoritarian.

With the dissolution of the Soviet Union, 15 independent states appeared on the map. The Russian Federation, the largest of these and the largest nation on Earth in area, was generally regarded as the successor-state to the Soviet Union. Before the dissolution, the presidents of Russia, Ukraine, and Belarus formed the Commonwealth of Independent States (CIS), a loose confederation of independent states, but not all of the former Soviet states joined—the Baltic states, for example, refused to have anything to do with the organization—and the CIS became largely meaningless.

The political system of Russia was initially based on the Congress of People's Deputies and a two-chamber Supreme Soviet. The Communist Party had been banned in August 1991 (although a new Russian Communist Party reorganized after 1991); at the same time, the KGB, the security police, had been disbanded, although a new security police force was later formed; and cities named for Communist leaders, such as Leningrad and Sverdlovsk, had returned to their original names. Newly independent Russia appeared to have rejected its Soviet past.

President Boris Yeltsin (1931–2007; in office as president of Russia 1991–1999) was the republic's chief of state, but confrontation soon occurred between the president and the legislature. The disagreement concerned possible solutions for Russia's deep economic crisis. Yeltsin and his government planned to reform the economy, introducing a free market and removing state control. From January 1992, controls on prices were ended, allowing true market prices for the first time in more than seven decades. The reform was economically painful for the people: the production of essential goods substantially declined, while prices and inflation rose. Within a couple of years, the standard of living had decreased to 50 percent of that in 1990. Consequently, the majority of deputies in the Supreme Soviet sought a return to the previous state-controlled system. In April 1993, the Congress initiated a referendum, a vote of no confidence in the president, but Yeltsin, and by extension his reforms, won 58.7 percent of the popular vote.

THE NEW GOVERNMENTAL SYSTEM

Yeltsin and his advisers prepared a new constitution, but the Supreme Soviet and the Congress delayed approval because the constitution would confer almost unlimited powers on the president. On September 21, 1993, Yeltsin proclaimed the dissolution of the legislature. In response, legislators barricaded themselves inside the White House, the legislative building in Moscow. With military support, Yeltsin besieged the building and used tanks and artillery to eject the legislators. The protesters surrendered. The new constitution, in force from late 1993, created a semipresidential system, with a powerful president as chief of state and a prime minister as head of government. Legislative power was vested in both the government and two chambers of the Federal Assembly.

Under Yeltsin, Russia accepted responsibility for settling the Soviet Union's external debts, and privatization largely shifted control of enterprises from state agencies to groups of individuals with links to the government and also to some with links to organized crime. Corruption of government officials became common, and many of the newly rich exported large sums in cash and assets outside the country. The downturn was accompanied by the collapse of social services, and the birthrate fell while the death rate rose suddenly and rapidly. The early and mid-1990s were also marked by extreme lawlessness. Criminal gangs, violence, and organized crime flourished.

CHECHNYA

Ethnic conflicts occurred in the north Caucasus, where conflicts took the form of separatist Islamist rebellions against the federal government. Chechen separatists tried to gain independence in 1991, but Yeltsin sent troops to confront the separatists, who controlled much of the region by 1994. From 1994 through 1996, in a fierce campaign (the First Chechen War), Russia struggled to regain Chechnya. An agreement in 1996 gave Chechnya considerable autonomy, but the situation deteriorated again in 1999 after a series of bombings in Russia that were blamed on Chechens. In the Second Chechen War, Russia conducted a short, brutal campaign to regain the devastated republic.

POLITICS IN THE NEW RUSSIA

In the mid-1990s, several political parties were represented in the new legislature: the (pro-government) Choice of Russia, the (ultranationalist, populist) Liberal Democratic Party of Russia, the Agrarian Party, and the Communist Party of Russia, as well as several small democratic, liberal and centrist parties. To varying degrees, the leading parties, therefore, were either populist or authoritarian.

The government carried out unpopular reforms, evoking general public dissatisfaction. The number of rich people dramatically increased, while the standard of living of the general population, and particularly of the poor and the retired, dropped. In August 1998, the Russian currency, the ruble, dramatically lost much of its value, wiping out most of the economic gains of the previous few years. The government admitted bankruptcy and defaulted on payment of $40 billion in ruble bonds. As a result, Yeltsin only narrowly won the elections in 1996, defeating the Communist leader, Gennady Zyuganov (born 1944).

PUTIN

On December 31, 1999, Yeltsin resigned from the presidency, handing the post to the recently appointed prime minister, Vladimir Putin (born 1952; in office as president 1999-2008 and as prime minister from 2008). Terrorist attacks, for example on apartment buildings in Moscow, carried out by Chechen separatists, shocked the Russian people. Putin promised to suppress the Chechen insurgency, and the strong action taken by the Russian army in Chechnya (which brought protests from the West) earned him popularity among Russians. Putin won the 2000 election without difficulty, in spite of his past career in the KGB. In October 2002, Chechen separatists seized a Moscow theater, threatening to kill all those inside. Putin ordered security forces to storm the theater, and during the operation some 130 hostages died, mostly as the result of inhaling gas released by security forces. Russian forces subsequently broke the resistance of separatists in Chechnya, although sporadic violence still occurs throughout the north Caucasus region.

In the twenty-first century under Putin, high oil prices permitted his government to pay off external debts. The living standards rose substantially, and the electorate expressed their confidence in his policies in the 2003 and 2007 legislative elections, when the United Russia Party, created by the government, received an overwhelming majority in the legislature. Liberal and democratic parties lost support, and their leadership was harassed. The government gradually became more authoritarian, and Putin moved to reassert central control over the country's regions by dividing the country into seven administrative districts, each of which would be overseen by a presidential appointee. During his rule, regional governors ceased to be elected and were, instead, appointed by him. Several media outlets, critical of the

Vladimir Putin (born 1952; in office as president 1999–2008 and as prime minister from 2008), on the left, shakes hands with Palestinian president Mahmoud Abbas (born 1935; in office from 2005) at the 2006 G8 summit in Saint Petersburg.

government, were closed, and criminal proceedings against numerous political figures were launched. Constitutional changes made it more difficult for smaller liberal and centrist parties to be elected to the legislature, and, as a result, none of the Western-style parties received a high enough percentage of the national vote to gain a seat in 2007. Other changes removed the right of independents to stand for election. Russia's brief experience of democracy was over.

In the presidential election in March 2008, Putin's protégé Dmitry Medvedev (born 1965) won. Putin assumed the office of prime minister and headed the party in power, United Russia, without even joining it. Subsequently, the constitutional arrangements of the country changed without recourse to legislation, as the office of premier became more powerful. This change was evidenced in a conflict in Georgia in 2008, when Georgian troops tried to retake the breakaway region of South Ossetia, in which Russian peacekeepers were based. Putin, rather than Medvedev, took control of the Russian reaction, and Russia increased the presence of its forces in South Ossetia and another Georgian breakaway region, Abkhazia, recognizing the independence of both.

S. KYULLENEN

CULTURAL EXPRESSION

Literature

Russian literature has a history of more than one thousand years, but two periods of outstanding achievement are recognized: nineteenth-century and modern Russian literature, both of which have attracted a wide international readership in translation.

The roots of Russian literature are traced to the first written lives of saints in the tenth century, written in Cyrillic script in the Old Russian language. At the same time, orders of religious services were written in Church Slavonic, a different but related language. One of the oldest pieces of Russian literature is the *Slovo o polku Igoreve* (The tale of Igor's campaign), a story of the failed campaign of Prince Igor of Novgorod Seversky against the nomadic armies of the Polovets. This and other old manuscripts were compiled into medieval Russian reading digests and, with the chronicles (*Letopis*), they were kept in Russian monasteries. Russian folk ballads (*bylinas*) survived in oral form in northern Russia to be rediscovered in the nineteenth century.

Medieval Russian written literature was largely religious or, to a lesser extent, historic in subject matter. The first use of colloquial Russian in written literature was by the cleric Avvakum (1620–1682) in his autobiography.

Undated statue of Maxim Gorky (1868–1936) in Nizhny Novgorod. He was born in the city, which was named Gorky between 1932 and 1990.

PETRINE LITERATURE

Reforms under Peter I (1672–1725; reigned as czar 1682–1721 and as emperor 1721–1725) included the simplification of the Cyrillic script, the introduction of public theater, and the publication of the first Russian newspaper. Poets and playwrights writing in the eighteenth century wrote in colloquial, rather than antique, Russian. Their number included dramatist Denis Fonvizin (1745–1792); poet and biographer Antioch Kantemir (1709–1744); poet Vasily Trediakovsky (1703–1769); scientist, artist, historian, and poet Mikhail Lomonosov (1711–1765); dramatist Alexander Sumarokov (1717–1777); and poet Gavriil Derzhavin (1743–1816). The works of these writers showed their knowledge and interest in Western literature, and Lomonosov and historian Nikolai Karamzin (1766–1821) are often credited with formulating the basis of the modern Russian literary language.

THE GOLDEN AGE

The Golden Age of Russian poetry, from 1820 through 1841, was inspired by the victory of the Russian army over French emperor Napoléon I (1769–1821; reigned 1804–1814 and 1815) in 1812–1815. Two leading Russian Romantic poets, Vasiliy Zhukovsky (1783–1852) and Alexander Pushkin (1799–1837), used Russian folk motifs in their poems and translated German, English, and French classics or gave free interpretations of them. Pushkin became Russia's most loved and famous poet. He produced a series of long poems, brilliant short poems, the historical tragedy *Boris Godunov* (1825; various translations), a series of short dramas, stories, and the famous novel in verse *Yevgeniy Onegin* (1833; *Eugene Onegin*, 1937). Pushkin developed a style of storytelling that became characteristic of Russian literature.

Mikhail Lermontov (1814–1841) is often considered the greatest Russian poet after Pushkin. His works include poems such as *Mtsyri* (The novice), short verses, several dramas, and the novel *Geroy nashego vremeni* (1841; *A Hero of Our Time*, 1958). Apart from a slim volume of poems, Lermontov was posthumously published. Lermontov's death in a duel symbolized the end of the Golden Age of Russian poetry, although he did not become popular until three decades later, when his works were published.

Literary critics such as Vissarion Belinsky (1811–1848) increasingly demanded that realistic prose address social issues. As result, novelists such as Nikolai Gogol (1809–1852) produced works that reflected life. Gogol, born in Ukraine but writing in Russian, wrote masterpieces such as the short story "Shinel" (1842; "The Overcoat," 1923) and his poem in prose *Myortvye dushi* (1842; The dead souls). Novelist and dramatist Ivan Turgenev (1818–1883) became famous for descriptions of new types of characters, such as young revolutionary nihilists.

Turgenev is best known for the novel *Ottsy i deti* (1842; *Fathers and Sons*; several translations).

Fyodor Dostoevsky (1821–1881) started his literary career with sentimental novels, such as *Bednye lyudi* (1846; Poor folk), but his trial and exile, for political activities, furthered his disillusionment with the government and made him reject revolutionary radicals as well. His study of the psychology of oppressed people is evident in novels such as *Prestupleniye i nakazaniye* (1866; *Crime and Punishment*, 1914) and *Bratya Karamavozy* (1879–1880; *The Brothers Karamazov*, 1912). Another Russian writer of the period, Leo Tolstoy (1828–1910), who was known for his realism, became famous for his long, detailed novels *Voyna i mir* (1865–1869; *War and Peace*, 1904) and *Anna Karenina* (1875–1877; translated 1901).

Anton Chekhov (1860–1904) initially gained a reputation in the 1890s as a short-story writer. Later, he wrote major plays, including *Chayka* (1896; *The Seagull*, 1912), *Tri sestry* (1900; *The Three Sisters*, 1923), and *Vishnevy sad* (1904; *The Cherry Orchard*, 1923).

THE SILVER AGE

The first two decades of the twentieth century are known as the Silver Age of Russian poetry. Valery Bryusov (1873–1924) and Alexander Block (1880–1921) started as symbolists, while Velimir Khlebnikov (1885–1922) and Vladimir Mayakovsky (1893–1930) countered by promoting a new trend known as Futurism. At the same time, a short-lived movement called Acmeist poetry, which promoted direct expression through images, flourished, led by Nikolay Gumilev (1886–1921), Osip Mandelshtam (1891–1938), and Anna Akhmatova (1889–1966). Among a group known as peasant poets, Sergey Yesenin (1895–1925) became known for his lyrical descriptions of the simple pastoral life of Russian villages.

THE REVOLUTION AND WRITERS UNDER COMMUNISM

Soon after the October 1917 Revolution, the Silver Age of Russian poetry ended in a period of political terror and the emigration of many Russian authors. Among many others, Vladimir Nabokov (1899–1977) emigrated from revolutionary Russia to the West and turned from poetry writing to prose. He also started translating his novels into English.

Novelist Maxim Gorky (1868–1936) became the favorite author of Soviet dictator Joseph Stalin (1879–1953; leader of the Soviet Communist Party and effectively ruler of Russia 1922–1953). Popular across the Soviet Union, Gorky defined the literary style known as Socialist Realism in 1932. After the revolution, he lived outside Russia from 1921 to 1929 and, after returning, was not permitted to leave. Another novelist, Ivan Bunin (1870–1953), did not accept the new Communist system and emigrated. Bunin became the first Russian to win the Nobel Prize for Literature in 1933.

Censorship of literature under Communism led to the publication of many less compelling works. As a result, a clandestine Soviet literature emerged in the 1930s. Daniil Kharms (1905–1942) of the Leningrad-based Association for Real Art (OBERIU, formed in 1927) wrote poetry and prose close to English and American Absurdism of the time. Nikolai Zabolotsky (1903–1958) produced grotesque poems but later turned to philosophical poetry. Mikhail Bulgakov (1891–1940), a playwright, novelist, and story-writer—known for his novel *Belaya gvardia* (1925; *The White Guard*, 1966)—did not see his most famous novel, *Master i Margarita* (1966; *The Master and Margarita*, 1966), published during his lifetime.

The late Soviet period saw the mass publication of world and Russian and Soviet classics, especially the works of Mikhail Sholokhov, best known for *Tikhii Don* (1928–40; *And Quiet Flows the Don*, 1934 and 1940). This promoted the careers of many talented, and some less-gifted but politically accepted, writers. However, censorship and ideological control, tightened after the Thaw under Leonid Brezhnev's rule from 1964 through 1982, led many talented authors into an underground literature, where critical, ironic and, sometimes, modernist novels and stories were covertly printed and circulated as *samizdat* (underground) literature; many writers also resorted to publishing their work abroad (*tamizdat*).

Alexander Solzhenitsyn (1918–2008) openly criticized the Stalinist past of the Soviet Union, for example, in the novella *Odin den' Ivana Denisovicha* (1962; *One Day in the Life of Ivan Denisovitch*, 1976), which was published with express consent of Nikita Khrushchev during the Thaw period (1956–1964). He was imprisoned in the GULAG system then expelled from the Soviet Union (1976) but continued to write realistic fiction and concentrated on collecting and publishing a history of political prisons in Russia (1976; *The Gulag Archipelago*), published in the West but then circulated in the Soviet Union as *samizdat* (self-published) literature.

MODERN RUSSIAN LITERATURE

The collapse of the Soviet Union ended the period of strict political and moral censorship. Authors, like Victor Pelevin (born 1962) and Vladimir Sorokin (born 1955), parodied the Soviet past in their works, defining a style called "sots-art", and offering caricatures of previous ideological rules and fantastic realism reflecting Soviet life. Translator and critic Grigory Chkhartishvili (pen name Boris Akunin; born 1956) started several literary projects that helped reawaken popular interest in literature, excelling at crime stories set in nineteenth-century Russia. The detective genre rose to the top of bestseller lists, with writers such as Alexandra Marinina, Darya Dontsova and Polina Dashkova, representing the most popular writers of the twenty-first century.

I. KOTIN

Dance

Russian folk dances developed from agricultural rites and rituals connected with festivals through the year, such as the harvest. Some early dances were linked to the pre-Christian cult of fertility. These traditions survived periods of persecution by the Russian Orthodox Church as well as neglect during part of the nineteenth and twentieth centuries. However, in Soviet times, there was considerable renewed interest in traditional dance as a people's culture. As a result, Russian folk dance is now part of the national folk culture, preserved and researched, and (until 1991) generously sponsored by the state. Russia has a number of high-profile traditional dance companies such as Beryozka, Barinya, the National Russian Dance Show, the Moiseyev Dance Company, and Russkaya Plyasovaya. It was, however, classical ballet rather than folk dances that won international acclaim for Russian dance.

Russia made a great contribution to the development of world ballet. Western ballet was introduced to Russia in the time of Alexis I (1629–1676; reigned 1645–1676), the father of Peter I (the Great; 1672–1725; reigned as czar 1682–1721 and as emperor 1721–1725). Peter the Great made theatrical performance a public event and, by the 1730s, foreign ballet companies were performing in Saint Petersburg, at the time Russia's new national capital. In 1734, the first ballet school was founded in the city.

In the nineteenth century, Russian ballet was dominated by French and Italian dancers and choreographers. Ivan Valberkh (1766–1819) was the first Russian-born choreographer and the first ballet master trained in Saint Petersburg. For fifty years, French choreographer Marius Petipa (1818–1910) was the ballet master of Saint Petersburg, where he directed the Imperial Ballet. The performances he devised included ballets to the music of Russian composer Pyotr Tchaikovsky (1840–1893): *Swan Lake* (1875/76), *Sleeping Beauty* (1888/89), and *The Nutcracker* (1891/92), which became the three great works of the classical ballet canon. Petipa is generally regarded as the founder of the Russian classical style of ballet.

In the early twentieth century, another Russian composer, Igor Stravinsky (1882–1971), created music for the ballets *The Firebird* (1910), *Petrushka* (1911), and *The Rite of Spring* (1913). The latter, with its innovative choreography and modern music, sharply divided critics and audiences when it was first performed. Stravinsky wrote for ballet impresario Sergei Diaghilev (1872–1929), who invited Russian artist Alexander Benois (1870–1960) to design sets and costumes. Diaghilev and his company, Ballets Russes, staged acclaimed performances across Europe and decided to stay in exile after World War I (1914–1918) broke out. Diaghilev's favorite Russian dancers, Anna Pavlova (1881–1931), who created the chief role in *Les Sylphides*, and Vaclav Nijinsky (1889–1950), for whom the ballets *Petrushka* and *Scheherazade* were created, did much to establish the reputation of Russian ballet in Europe. Diaghilev's protégé, Russian-Georgian émigré George Balanchine (1904–1983), founded the New York City Ballet in 1948.

After the Russian Revolution in 1917, the Soviet government was initially hostile toward ballet, perceiving it as an elite czarist relic. However, by the late 1920s, the Communist authorities began to support the ballet schools and theaters in Moscow and Leningrad, promoting patriotic and revolutionary ballets that reflected the ideology of the state. In the 1930s, Russian-Soviet ballet returned to the classical style of performances, and ballerinas, such as Galina Ulanova (1910–1998), became world-famous.

After World War II (1939–1945), artists such as Maya Plisetskaya (born 1925), who was known for her ability to integrate dance and acting, and choreographers such as Yuri Grigorovich (born 1927), whose ballets were characteristically spectacular, helped maintain Russian ballet as arguably the finest in the world. In the 1960s, the Bolshoi Theater Company (from Moscow) and the Kirov Ballet Company (from Leningrad) started to tour worldwide. Despite the defection to the West of leading ballet dancers—Rudolf Nureyev (1938–1993), who defected in 1961; Natalia Makarova (born 1940), defected 1970; Mikhail Baryshnikov (born 1948), defected 1974; and Alexander Godunov (1949–1995), defected 1979—Soviet ballet companies continued to tour, enjoying success owing to the flawless technique of their dancers. Soviet ballet had a strong base, including ballet theaters in all major cities and many ballet schools, most famously the Vaganova ballet school in Leningrad.

With the collapse of the Soviet Union in 1991, Russian ballet companies received a shock when their state support was terminated. Many dancers, including some not of the first rank, went to the West to work, but the major companies survived and soon prospered again. The Moscow Bolshoi and Saint Petersburg Mariinsky (formerly the Kirov, when Saint Petersburg was known as Leningrad) companies have retained their leading positions in world ballet.

Until 1991, the Mariinsky Ballet Company of Saint Petersburg was known as the Kirov Ballet, the name that it continues to use when performing internationally.

Festivals and Ceremonies

The holidays and festivals celebrated in modern Russia reflect the country's history: some mark ancient traditions; others are of Christian origin; yet others were introduced under Communism.

The celebration of Maslenitsa (the week before Lent) in a Russian village concludes with the burning of a straw effigy of Lady Maslenitsa, a tradition dating back to pre-Christian times.

The major religious festivals celebrated in Russia are not held on the same date as they are in Catholic and Protestant countries. The Russian Orthodox Church retains the older Julian Calendar rather than the Gregorian calendar, which was adopted across most of Europe in the sixteenth century and in Russia, for secular purposes, in 1921. The Julian calendar now runs about two weeks apart from the Gregorian calendar.

WINTER HOLIDAYS

January 1, New Year's Day, is the main public holiday of the year in Russia. In many ways, the holiday replaced Christmas in the period of the Soviet Union. In the 1930s, the character Ded Moroz (Father Frost) was introduced as a politically acceptable alternative to the Western Santa Claus. Small children believe that Father Frost—who has a similar appearance to Santa Claus but is depicted wearing a blue fur coat—brings them presents on New Year's Eve. A New Year tree, like a Christmas tree, is decorated for the festival in every home and in most workplaces.

On January 7, Orthodox Christmas is celebrated and traditional Russian Orthodox church services are held. The festival is marked to a lesser extent than New Year's Day but is a public holiday. Old New Year's Day is celebrated a week later but is not a public holiday.

The third public holiday of the year is the Day of the Defender of the Fatherland on February 23. This holiday honors those who served or are serving in Russia's armed forces. The date is the anniversary of the first victory of the Red Army over German forces in 1918, during World War I (1914–1918). The military character of the holiday is now diminished from Soviet times, when the holiday was called Red Army Day. It is a custom on this day to congratulate all the men and boys in a family and to give them a present.

SPRING HOLIDAYS

March 8 is International Women's Day and is marked by giving mothers, sisters, and other female relatives gifts and flowers. The holiday is similar in some respects to Mother's Day and Valentine's Day. In modern times, the Western custom of Valentine's Day is also becoming popular in Russia.

Maslenitsa (Shrove Tuesday) is a pre-Lenten celebration of pagan origin. It celebrates the end of winter and welcomes the spring sun. The festival, which is traditionally marked by eating blinis (pancakes), is not a public holiday. Easter, too, is not a public holiday, but practicing Christians attend church, and many people follow ancient traditions of exchanging kisses and Easter eggs. Easter paskha (a dish made of flour, eggs, honey, curds, dried fruits and nuts) and kulichi (Easter breads) are prepared.

May 1 is Spring and Labor Day. In Communist times, the holiday was called the International Day of the Solidarity of Working People and was marked by huge parades. May 9, Victory Day, is still an important national celebration. This marks the end of World War II (1939–1945) and the surrender of German forces. Ceremonies of remembrance for those who were killed in the conflict are held, and a large military parade is held in Moscow.

Sports

Russian folk sports, such as various forms of wrestling, boxing, and ice skating, had been a popular form of entertainment in both urban and rural Russia before the twentieth century. The revival of the Olympic movement in the West in 1896 spurred an interest in sports in Russia, and Russia competed in the early revived games. However, the greatest encouragement to the promotion of sports was the perception under Communism of the importance of sports as physical training for the population. Through the 1920s, the Soviet Union prepared the nation for defense and encouraged interest in sports to promote fitness. In the Soviet Union in the 1930s through 1950s, track and field and shooting became an integral part of training youths for military service.

From the 1930s, soccer was under state protection, and various soccer clubs enjoyed sponsorship from government ministries. The clubs Dinamo Kiev and Dinamo Moscow were funded by the NKVD (People's Commissariat of Internal Affairs, the security police), while the CSKA (Central Sports Club of the Army) was the Soviet Army soccer club. Later, the system of state sponsorship was reduced as the Soviet economy declined.

In modern times, since the collapse of the Soviet Union and the end of Communism, soccer clubs are professional in the top divisions of the national leagues. The principal competition is the 16-member Premier League, whose most successful teams are CSKA Moscow, Spartak Moscow, and Zenit Saint Petersburg. Many leading Russian players now play abroad, where financial rewards are greater. The national team is well supported but has had proportionately less success in international competitions than the size of the nation's population might suggest.

The Soviet regime regarded success in international sports as politically important, and sports were heavily promoted for propaganda purposes. Participation in the Olympic Games was an important part of this image. The Soviet Union took part in the Olympics for the first time in 1952 in Helsinki, Finland, where 22 gold, 30 silver, and 19 bronze medals were won by Soviet athletes. After that, the Soviet team was normally first in the medal table in the Olympic Games, and Soviet athletes were rewarded by the state for their contribution to Soviet prestige abroad. Soviet athletes were particularly successful in track and field, gymnastics, hockey, weightlifting, and figure skating.

Among the greatest Soviet athletes were Larisa Latynina (born 1934), who won a total of 18 medals, including 9 golds, in Olympic gymnastics. In the same sport, Nikolay Andrianov (born 1952) won 15 Olympic medals, including 7 golds; Boris Shakhlin (1932–2008) won 13 Olympic medals; and Victor Chukarin (1921–1984) won 11 Olympic medals, including 7 golds.

The hockey team of the Soviet Union was for decades the winner of the gold medal at the Olympics as well as being world champions. Famous Russian hockey players include Vyacheslav Starshinov (born 1940), Valery Kharlamov (1948–1981), Alexander Yakushev (born 1947), and Vladislav Tretyak (born 1952).

Soviet, and now Russian, competitors have long dominated international figure skating. Pairs skater Irina Rodnina (born 1949) is the only figure skater to have won 10 successive world championships (1969–1978) and three successive Olympic Games. Other internationally known Russian figure skaters include Alexander Zaytsev (born 1952) and Igor Bobrin (born 1953). Russia also won many international weightlifting competitions, and Vasiliy Alekseyev (born 1942), who set 80 world records, is sometimes considered the greatest super-heavyweight weightlifter in history.

However, Soviet athletes became victims of Soviet policies, as Western countries boycotted the Moscow Olympic Games of 1980 because of the Soviet invasion of Afghanistan and the Soviets ignored the next Olympic Games in Los Angeles. The Soviets organized alternative Goodwill or Friendship Games, but they proved to be short-lived.

Russians are also prominent in basketball and chess as well as in cross-country skiing and pentathlon events. Although chess was popular in prerevolutionary times, when Mikhail Chigorin (1850–1908) was a major player, it was under the Soviet Union that Russian chess players became dominant. The most successful were Mikhail Botvinnik (1911–1995), Boris Spassky (born 1937), Anatoly Karpov (born 1951), and Garry Kasparov (born 1963). In modern times, tennis has become popular, thanks to the success of players such as Maria Sharapova (born 1987).

Maria Sharapova (born 1987) won her first tennis Grand Slam title in 2004, aged only 17.

SUMMER AND FALL HOLIDAYS

Russia Day (June 12) is the National Day. The holiday celebrates the anniversary of the declaration of sovereignty by the legislature of the Russian Soviet Federative Socialist Republic in 1990, an event that preceded the collapse of the Soviet Union by 18 months. Unity Day, November 4, marks the uprising of the Muscovites against Polish invaders in 1612. This holiday was introduced in 2005 to replace Revolution Day (November 7), which celebrated the seizure of power by the Communists in 1917. Russia's Catholics and Protestants celebrate Christmas on December 25. There are other local holidays—mainly Muslim, Jewish, and Buddhist celebrations—in the different autonomous republics and regions of Russia.

I. KOTIN

Food and Drink

Russian food is characterized by its hearty dishes and its reflection of the many different ethnic traditions within the country. In modern times, Russian cuisine probably owes less to Western recipes than almost any other cuisine in Europe.

Russian food is generally considered tasty and, in its use of fresh, natural ingredients, is relatively nutritious, although it is particularly rich in calories. Many Russians still believe that the more calories their food contains, the better it is for them.

REGIONAL INFLUENCES

Russian cuisine became standardized with the Communist collectivization of agriculture in the 1930s, when cafeterias were established on communes and many local recipes were lost. The nation's cuisine also reflects some Western, particularly French, influences, but it owes even more to the ethnic cuisines of the former Soviet republics. Ukrainian borscht (beet soup) is now as Russian as *shchi* (cabbage soup). Shashlik (barbecued meat) from the Caucasus region and *pelmeni* (dumplings stuffed with meat), a Siberian recipe, are popular parts of the Russian diet.

Russian cuisine does not generally include foreign-style restaurant food dishes, such as pizza and curries, mostly owing to the fact that, until the 1990s, dining out was restricted to special occasions. Now, although dining out in restaurants that offer Italian, Indian, French, Chinese, and other cuisines, is more common, economic circumstances dictate that restaurant meals remain a privilege for more wealthy people in Russia. The introduction of various forms of fast food in modern Russia has not yet changed local eating habits. Russians even make fun of local fast food by calling fast-food kiosks that offer Russian rather than Western alternatives Blin-Donalds (combining blini and McDonalds).

MAIN MEALS

Russians usually eat three meals a day. In the morning, breakfast usually consists of kasha, or *grechka* (boiled buckwheat), semolina, or another cereal. In middle-class urban families, cornflakes are now popular. Other breakfast dishes may include bread and butter with cheese, sausages, or ham, and tea (usually without milk but with sugar) or coffee.

Lunch (*obed*) may be eaten between one and four in the afternoon and, if lunch is eaten late in the day, dinner is also late. Russians prefer to eat lunch at home, if possible, but often working people may eat in a cafeteria. Lunch generally consists of *zakuski* (a starter), which may be salads and bread, sometimes with fish. In celebration meals, caviar (the roe of the sturgeon) might be served in wealthy families, but this custom is relatively rare in modern times. A cheaper option is herring, served with a beet salad and mayonnaise.

The first course may be soup, which is often substantial and may be the main part of the meal. Borscht, in particular, is heavy. This thick soup is based on beef stock with added beets and other ingredients. It is, usually, a simpler variety of the *borscht* dish that the Ukrainians often claim to be their national dish. Other favorite soups include *shchi*, *rassolnik* (cucumber soup), *ukha* (fish soup), *gribnoy* (mushroom soup), and chicken soup. *Shchi* is

A traditional Russian tea urn, a samovar, with bubliks, which are similar to bagels.

based on meat stock with the addition of cabbage. Sometimes pickled cabbage is also added, in which case *shchi* is known as *kislie shchi*. Other varieties include *zelenie shchi* (made from young green cabbage) and *postnie shchi* (Lenten *shchi*), a pure vegetable soup that was traditionally made for consumption during Lent.

The next, or main, course usually comprises meat or fish served with potatoes and vegetables. Blinis (pancakes) are often part of the main course, but they also come in many varieties that are popular at festivals and are offered as fast food at kiosks, especially before Lent at the Maslenitsa festival. Blinis are commonly said to be shaped to resemble the sun, and, for parties, these "small suns" were baked in great numbers and counted not by their number but by the dimensions of the piles of blinis compared with the size of the human elbow (*lokot*). A smaller version of the blini, called the *oladyi*, is deep-fried in oil. *Tretye* (the third course of lunch or of dinner) is the *sladkoe* (dessert), which usually includes cakes, pies, or pastries, perhaps pirogi or small pies.

Uzhin (dinner) is usually a much less heavy meal than lunch. Dishes typically eaten at dinner are usually similar to those served at lunch, but the portions are normally smaller and the variety of dishes is generally far less. Tea is generally served with this meal.

DRINKS

Russian traditional drinks include vodka, *pivo* (beer), *kvas* (a fermented beverage), and *sbiten* (a nonalcoholic hot winter beverage). Outside Russia, vodka is the most famous Russian drink. The domestic consumption of vodka is huge, and alcoholism is a continuing and serious social problem for the nation. Vodka in Russia is usually served chilled, although rarely in cocktails. Straight vodka is still the favorite alcoholic drink of Russians, although *pertsovka* (pepper-flavored vodka), *limonnaya* (lemon vodka), and *okhotnichya* (ginger vodka) are also popular. In modern times, the consumption of beer has greatly increased in Russia (particularly among younger men), threatening the traditional domination of vodka. This trend is, in part, welcomed by the authorities, in the hopes that it may lead to a decrease in the excessive consumption of vodka. Local brands of beer, such as Baltika and Tinkoff, are among the most popular, although foreign brands, like Carlsberg and Tuborg, are now also widely available in Russia.

Kasha is buckwheat, commonly eaten as a side dish or for breakfast.

Wines are not widely consumed when compared with most other European countries. In the Soviet era, Russians used to buy wines from the Soviet republics of Georgia and Moldavia (modern Moldova), and, although the quantities consumed in Russia have decreased since these countries became independent with the collapse of the Soviet Union in 1991, Georgian and Moldovan wines are still popular. Crimean fortified wines (particularly *massandra*) were also popular in the time of the Soviet Union, but, now, partly in order to support Russia's own wine producers, the Russian government has promoted wine production in southern Russia. In modern times, Tsimlyanskoe sparkling wines from the Novorossiysk region are increasingly appreciated for their quality.

Mineral water, milk, *kefir* (soured milk), and fruit juices are healthier alternatives chosen by many Russians. *Kvas* is a national beverage made by the alcoholic fermentation of wheat, rye, and barley with the addition of sugar, fruit, or berries. The cheapest and the most popular variety of *kvas* is based on dried rye bread. One of the most popular types of *kvas* is flavored with raspberries. The percentage of alcohol in kvas is so low (1–2 percent) that it is consumed by people of all ages, and it is commonly served to children. A popular nonalcoholic beverage known as *sbiten* is made by adding honey, ginger, and spices to hot water. *Sbiten* and *med* (a low-alcohol beverage with honey, served hot or chilled) both lost popularity to tea and beer in the early twentieth century, but both have started to regain a place in the national diet in modern times.

I. KOTIN

DAILY LIFE

Religion

After the seizure of power by the Communists in Russia in 1917 and the establishment of the Soviet Union in 1922, public policy decreed scientific atheism. Since the collapse of Communism in 1991, a religious revival has occurred.

There are no state statistics in Russia concerning the numbers of followers of different religions. The only official data records the number of registered places of worship: in 2006, there were 12,214 Russian Orthodox churches and 3,668 Islamic and 6,631 other places of worship registered with the Ministry of Justice. The state recorded 1,486 Pentecostal places of worship, 965 Baptist churches, 652 Seventh-Day Adventist meeting places, 228 Lutheran churches, and 251 Roman Catholic churches.

Estimates of the numbers of followers of different religions in Russia vary greatly. In modern times, some 16 percent of the population belongs to the Russian Orthodox Church, practicing their religion to a greater or lesser extent. However, around 70 percent of the population identifies with the Russian Orthodox culture and may describe themselves as Orthodox for some purposes. (Some estimates place the number of practicing Orthodox Christians as low as 5 percent.) At the same time,

The Cathedral of Christ the Savior in Moscow was demolished during Stalin's rule and reconstructed between 1990 and 2000, after the revival of interest in religion in modern Russia.

65–70 percent of Russians are nonreligious (atheists and agnostics) or nominal Christians. Sunni Islam accounts for 10–15 percent of the Russian population. Evangelical Christians, Baptists, Roman Catholics, Old Believers, and other Christians account for 2 percent.

ORTHODOX CHRISTIANITY

Vladimir I (c. 958–1015; reigned 980–1015), ruler of Kievan Rus, adopted Orthodox Christianity as the state religion in 988 CE. The Orthodox Church remained the established religion until 1918. As the oldest established religion in the Russian Empire, Orthodox Christianity was represented in all spheres of public and social life. Other religions, that is, those of non-Russian nations within the empire (such as the Muslim Kazakhs and Buddhist Buryats), were initially considered to be targets for Orthodox missionaries.

Patriarch Nikon (1605–1681), head of the Russian Orthodox Church, began important reforms in the middle of the seventeenth century. He summoned synods to consider reforms that adapted original Byzantine practices. Nikon introduced new service books and worship and introduced styles of icons and church buildings that were closer to those of the original Orthodox traditions. As a result, a significant number of priests and congregations, later called Old Believers, seceded from the Russian Orthodox Church because they disagreed with the reforms. In 2006, there were 285 Old Believers' churches registered.

According to a decree of religious tolerance, published by Empress Catherine II the Great (1729–1796; reigned 1762–1796) in 1773, Orthodox clergy were prohibited from interfering in the affairs of other religious groups. In April 1905, a state edict guaranteed religious freedom for all non-Orthodox believers.

One of the basic tenets of the Communist Party, which came to power in 1917, was a struggle against religion, which was considered by Karl Marx (1818–1883), German founder of Communism, to be "the opiate of the people." As a result, in 1918, the Soviet authorities disestablished the Russian Orthodox

Church and deprived it, along with all other religious organizations, of all their rights and properties and prohibited them from any role in education. A campaign of militant atheism began. Many churches—as well as synagogues, mosques, and Buddhist temples—were closed or destroyed. For example, some eight thousand Russian Orthodox churches were closed in 1937 alone.

Many Orthodox clerics had to leave Russia because of Communist persecution. In the 1920s, the exiles founded the Russian Orthodox Church Outside of Russia. However, in 2007, under the Act of Canonical Communion with the Moscow patriarchate, the Russian Orthodox Church Outside of Russia became a semiautonomous part of the Russian Orthodox Church.

In 1927, the Russian Orthodox Church within Russia achieved an understanding with the state. Acting head of the church, later patriarch, Sergius I (1867–1944; in office as acting head 1925–1943 and as patriarch 1943–1944) acknowledged loyalty to the state in return for limited tolerance. This led to the separation of what became known as the Catacomb Churches, which refused to cooperate with the Communists and, largely, went underground.

A slight relaxation of persecution occurred during World War II (1939–1945), at a time when national unity was essential. The leaders of the Russian Orthodox Church promised a policy of cooperation with the Soviet government, and, as a result, they were allowed to open the Moscow Theological Seminary and Academy, some imprisoned clerics were released, and many of the church's properties were returned. The most significant result was the election of a new patriarch, Sergius I. Subsequently however, a new wave of oppression was started by Nikita Khrushchev (1894–1971; in office as general secretary of the Communist Party and effective ruler of the Soviet Union 1953–1964 and as prime minister 1958–1964) in the late 1950s. During reforms under Mikhail Gorbachev (born 1931; in office as general secretary of the Communist Party 1985–1991 and as chief of state and later president 1988–1991), the policy of perestroika (reconstruction) brought an end to state persecution of religion, and a religious revival began. In 1991, a law that guaranteed freedom of religion was adopted.

ISLAM

Islam is the second-largest religion in Russia in terms of adherents. Muslims in Russia, nearly all Sunnis (the largest branch of Islam worldwide), are almost entirely members of ethnic minorities. Some 2 percent of Russian Muslims are Shias (members of the smaller main branch of Islam), while some Muslims in the Caucasus are Sufis (Muslims who emphasize a

A mosque in Elabuga, Tatarstan; the majority of the republic's population are Sunni Muslims.

direct personal experience of God). Russian Muslims include Tatars, who descend from Muslims who settled the Volga-Ural region (mostly in what are now Tatarstan and Bashkortostan) in the Middle Ages, as well as various peoples, such as the Chechens, in the northern Caucasus region. They also include residents of Moscow, Saint Petersburg, and western Siberia.

Islam in Russia has a long history, beginning with the conquest of the Kazan, Astrakhan, and Siberian khanates by the Russians in the middle of the sixteenth century. Later, in the eighteenth and nineteenth centuries, the Crimean khanate and north Caucasus were incorporated into Russia, followed by Central Asia. Like other religions in Russia, Islam was persecuted in Soviet times, but, after 1991, rights were restored to Islamic organizations. In 2006, according to the Ministry of Hajj of Saudi Arabia, some 18,000 Russian Muslims attended the pilgrimage to Mecca that year.

JUDAISM

The Jewish population of Russia is a fraction of its former size; some perished in World War II in the Holocaust and, after 1945, Judaism suffered persecution within the Soviet Union. In the 1980s, when reforms allowed emigration, and in the 1990s, after the collapse of the Soviet Union, more than half of Russia's Jews left the country, most for Israel but some for the United States and Germany. In modern times, there are 284 registered Jewish synagogues in Russia, and the nation still has one of the larger Jewish populations in Europe. The majority belong to Orthodox congregations, mostly Hasidic (a sect of Jewish mystics founded in Poland in the eighteenth century), and are united in the Federation of Jewish Communities of Russia. Since the end of the rigid Communist state system, anti-Semitism has increased in Russian life.

BUDDHISM

Buddhism is one of the oldest religions in Russia. Buddhist regions in Siberia and toward the Pacific coast region were included in Russia in the sixteenth century. In modern times, three of Russia's autonomous republics have Buddhist majorities: Buryatia and Tuva in southern Siberia and Kalmykia, which is situated in the Volga region. Kalmykia is the only European Buddhist region. The official center of Russian Buddhists is the Ivolginsky *datsan* (monastery) in Buryatia, and, in modern times, there are 197 registered Buddhist places of worship in Russia. The main form of Buddhism practiced in Russia is the Gelukpa school of Tibetan Buddhism.

A. SOKOLOVA

Family and Society

Russia is a multiethnic state whose social structures still owe much to seven decades of Communist dictatorship in the twentieth century.

The Russian Federation is home to some 160 different ethnicities. Europeans and Caucasian peoples account for 89 percent of the population, of which Russians form 80 percent; Ukrainians 2 percent; Chechens 1 percent; Armenians, Belarussians (also given as Belarusians), Germans, Ossetians, Moldovans, and other European and Caucasian peoples another 4 percent. Various Turkic peoples form 8 percent of the population of Russia, with Tatars accounting for 4 percent; Bashkirs 1 percent; Chuvash people 1 percent; and Kazakhs, Azeris, Yakuts, and others 2 percent. Various Asian peoples form another 3 percent of the Russian population, with Buryats, Mongols, Koreans, and Kalmyks among the largest groups. Significant ethnic minorities generally have their own autonomous republic or region within the Russian Federation, but some of these groups do not form a majority within the republic to which they, generally, give their name. For example, Tatars account for 48 percent of the population of Tatarstan and Bashkirs only 22 percent of the population of Bashkortostan.

THE FAMILY AND THE LAW

Russians consider the family the main unit of the society. Pre-revolutionary Russia was a patriarchal society, and, in imperial times (before 1917), there was a strict behavioral code, emphasizing gender roles. This was enforced by imperial decrees; for example, Article 107 of the Marriage Code decreed the subordinate status of wives and their obedience and loyalty to their husbands. However, the industrialization of Russia and Russia's involvement in wars—the Russo-Japanese War (1904–1905) and World War I (1914–1918)—forced large numbers of husbands to leave their families for years. Consequently, many patriarchal families collapsed, reducing the impact of these codes.

The Russian Revolution of October 1917 was another blow to the family structure. The December 1917 Marriage and Divorce Decree of the Soviet government simplified both marriage and divorce procedures. In 1920, abortions were legalized by the Soviet state. The revolutionaries included the first Soviet female commissar, Alexandra Kollontay (1872–1952), commissar for social welfare in the Soviet government, who urged the people to get rid of the burden of family. Initially, this idea became part of the general Communist vision of common property and feminism. However, when their power was established, the Soviet authorities again felt the need to promote the family as the unit of society.

In Soviet times, women were, in theory, equal to men in rights, responsibilities, and employment opportunities. However, women bore the bulk of responsibilities for household work. In the 1930s, women were guaranteed equal pay and voting rights, but their social freedom was limited.

Much changed with World War II (1939–1945), when most homes were deprived of the male family head, conscripted into the armed forces. Large numbers of Soviet soldiers were killed, and many women found themselves as head of the family, not only during the war but afterward.

In the postwar period, living conditions for many families were poor and overcrowded. As a result, the number of children in families fell. By 1970, the average size of the Soviet family was 3.1 children, but through the last quarter of the twentieth century and into the twenty-first century, the birthrate in Russia has continued to decline. In modern times, Russian women on average give birth to 1.4 children.

MARRIAGE AND DIVORCE

Marriage in the Soviet Union was often not long-lasting. In the 1980s, the Soviet Union had the second-largest number of divorces in the world after the United States. The main reasons for divorce were infidelity and alcoholism of husbands, but it was often crowded housing that created the strains that led to the collapse of families. Generally, women remained custodians of their children after divorce. Despite the high divorce rate, Russian society was—and to some extent still is—critical of divorce. In modern times, Russia still has a high rate of marriage failure.

Post-Soviet Russian society developed more tolerance toward divorced and unregistered unions. Russian society is, however, extremely hostile toward sexual minorities and same-sex couples. There has been a trend toward young people not marrying at all, although the rise of a middle class in Russia has supported a rise in the perceived value of married life and of raising children. The government of Russia proclaimed 2008 the Year of the Family and promoted programs for familial support, housing, health care, and education, recognizing, in modern times, the importance of the family to society as a whole.

URBANIZATION

Under Communism, the collectivization of property in the 1920s and 1930s in rural areas led to shortages, starvation, and huge

Russia has a declining birthrate, and many families now have only one child.

loss of life, causing a massive population migration from villages to cities. Urban society was, in many ways, easier for the Soviet authorities to shape. At the same time, enforced movements of population, either the exile of political dissidents and their families, or the movement of labor to new industrial enterprises, also changed the distribution of population. These population movements often involved the movement of different peoples from across the Soviet Union to the cities. Urbanization also had an effect upon population increase because the fertility rate of the urban population was lower than that in rural areas.

POPULATION DECLINE

A falling birthrate is one element in a scenario that has led to a decline in the population of the Russian Federation. Since the collapse of the Soviet Union, health care standards have fallen and, partly as a result, life expectancy, particularly the life expectancy of Russian men, has declined. In 2007, while Russian women had a life expectancy of 73.1 years, Russian men lived, on average, to only 59.2 years. Alcoholism plays a major role in the decrease of life expectancy for Russian men, many of whom drink large quantities of vodka. One-third of all male deaths in Russia are alcohol-related, and the Russian authorities acknowledge this major social problem.

Changing expectations and an increase in employment opportunities in the cities, have led in modern times to a huge redistribution in population. Many younger people have left the countryside to live and work in the cities, enjoying a right that, in Soviet times, they would not have had because residence in cities, such as Moscow, required a permit. As a result, many villages are practically deserted, home to only a few elderly women. By 2007, some 34,000 villages across Russia were home to fewer than 10 people, mostly elderly women. The absence of elderly men is a common feature in many villages.

At the same time, many Russians have emigrated to work abroad, throughout Europe and farther afield. This freedom to travel did not exist in Soviet times and, consequently, many people have embraced the novelty and emigrated. However, many ethnic Russians left other former Soviet republics that gained their independence in 1991 and relocated to Russia, although not in numbers large enough to balance the outflow of people from Russia. Early in the twenty-first century, a low birthrate, a death rate that exceeds the birthrate, and emigration result in a declining national population; the population of the Russian Federation is decreasing by 0.5 percent a year. In 2006, Russia had a population of 142,754,000, whereas, in 2000, it had been 145,470,000 and, in 1991, 148,542,000. It is estimated that, by 2025, the population of Russia will be in the region of 135,000,000.

I. KOTIN

Health and Welfare

In the 1970s and 1980s, the citizens of the Soviet Union enjoyed free health care and a comprehensive (but not generous) welfare state. Economic difficulties and the collapse of the Soviet system in 1991 brought the end of this network of state support and, although health care provision and social security remain, they are available at a much reduced level.

Modern Russia inherited health care and welfare systems from the Soviet Union. However, these systems have faced a multidimensional challenge since the collapse of the Soviet Union, including the huge financial costs of a transitional period as an independent Russian Federation emerged; more than one severe financial crisis that drastically reduced the ability of the state to provide health care and welfare payments; a large inflow of migrants (ethnic Russians relocating from other former Soviet republics); and the loss of parts of the former Soviet infrastructure. At the same time, the state had also to meet the growing demands of an aging population, as the birthrate fell and many younger people went abroad to work and live.

HEALTH CARE

The Russian constitution repeats paragraphs of Soviet law, giving guarantees of universal, free health care for every citizen. This provision was not upheld even in the Soviet Union, and, in modern times, the Russian Federation allocates proportionately fewer resources to health care than the Soviet Union did. The health care system suffers from underinvestment, and much of the infrastructure needs replacing. Many local and regional hospitals lack sufficient modern equipment, although large city hospitals have better facilities. In 2008, the authorities invested in creating eight major high-tech medical centers and renewing equipment such as X-ray machines and ambulances. However, many local hospitals lack equipment and drugs: for example, many patients with diabetes are not able to receive necessary drugs in time. At the same time, many elite facilities, like high-class health care at spa resorts, are not available to the majority of the population, while the few who have access to these luxury services, usually owing to personal contacts, pay only 10 percent or less for costly treatment. Since the collapse of the Soviet Union, many doctors have left the state medical centers because of underpayment or nonpayment of salaries.

By 2008, declining standards of health care, along with chronic alcoholism among Russian men—one-third of all Russian male deaths are alcohol related—and an unhealthy style of living, led to a large decline in life expectancy in Russia. The trend was exacerbated by tobacco smoking, violent crimes, traffic accidents because of careless driving, and violation of safety measures in the workplace. Consequently, in 2007,

although Russian women had a life expectancy of 73.1 years, Russian men lived, on average, to only 59.2 years.

Russians contract a number of diseases that are characteristic of modern industrial and postindustrial societies, although to a greater extent than in many developed countries. Some of these diseases have their roots in lifestyles; for example, more than 50 percent of all deaths in Russia are caused by heart disease. One in ten Russians contract cardiovascular diseases, owing to a poor environment, an unhealthy diet and lack of exercise, and lack of medical care. As a result, the nation has a high mortality rate and a diminishing, aging population. Other major health problems include alcohol-related injury and poisoning, sharply increasing rates of HIV/AIDS infection, and a resurgence of resistant strains of tuberculosis (TB).

REFORMS

The Russian health care system is, in theory, free, paid for by the state out of taxation and other revenue. Early in the twenty-first century, increases in expenditure (to improve infrastructure and to pay wage increases to staff) were paid for from oil revenues. However, patients and their families commonly pay bribes for better treatment and facilities, even for drugs, while those unable to pay must often go without necessary medicine. Corruption is endemic within the system, and it is estimated that corruption siphons off more than one-third of the health care budget at a local level in many places in Russia.

The nation faces the need for major reforms in health care. In Soviet times, there was a preoccupation with quantity, the number of patients treated. In modern times, the emphasis has switched to quality and the efficacy of treatment. There also has been a decline in the number of specialists and a concurrent program to encourage more doctors to enter general practice. This move has been criticized; although an increased number of general practitioners could improve primary care, a decrease in the number of specialists could deprive patients of more advanced treatments.

The state has decided to implement the financial reform of its health care and welfare obligations, beginning in 2006–2007, when pensioners and war veterans were told that some social services, including free travel and free medicines, were not available to them anymore. The end of some formerly free services and concessions were extremely unpopular among the general population.

WELFARE

The welfare system of the former Soviet Union catered to all sections of society; payments were not large, although adequate for a generally low standard of living. During the transitional period of Russia's economy toward a free market, following the breakup of the Soviet socialist system, a minority became wealthy, but the elderly, the handicapped, the homeless, and the unskilled were left behind. Many of these people are no longer sufficiently cared for by the state and have to rely upon charitable organizations. As well as failing to provide any coverage for sectors of the population, the current welfare system has other shortcomings: benefits are unavailable in many regions, and there is a disparity between shrinking revenue and growing demand.

As in the Soviet period, benefits in Russia are distributed through state agencies. Social security and welfare programs provide modest support for vulnerable segments of Russia's population: elderly pensioners, veterans, infants and children, expectant mothers, families with more than one child, invalids, and people with disabilities. These programs are inadequate, however, and a growing proportion of Russia's population lives in poverty. In 2007, some 15.7 percent of the population lived below the official poverty line.

Several governmental funds provide cash and social welfare. The Fund for Social Support provides assistance, but its many programs are now reduced to a modest monetary equivalent. The Pension Fund pays (small) pensions to retired state workers and finances some child allowances and other entitlements. The inefficiency of the Pension Fund forces the state to encourage working people to invest in private pension funds. However, these private funds are often risky investments, and elderly people generally prefer to rely on the government and the state Pension Fund.

There are also state maternity benefits, but these are now a one-time payment. Women with an employment contract are entitled to receive maternity leave from 70 days prior to giving birth until 70 days afterward. In 2007, to encourage childbearing in a society with a declining population, the state introduced a payment equivalent to $10,000 for mothers giving birth to second and subsequent children. This proved to be a successful encouragement, and the number of births did increase slightly.

The Social Insurance Fund is the source of payments to workers for sickness allowances and child allowances for children between the ages of 6 and 16. The fund is managed by the largest labor union in Russia, the Federation of Independent Trade Unions of Russia. The Unemployment Agency allows people to register for unemployment allowances and tries to find jobs for those registered. It usually offers only unskilled and low-paid jobs. However, many people in Russia are not unemployed but underemployed, and this uneconomic situation is yet to be adequately addressed. Low pay also remains a major problem. The welfare system does not cater to the homeless either; the hasty and uncontrolled privatization of accommodations left many people who were formerly paying rent without a place in which to live.

I. KOTIN

The temperate climate of Sochi in southwestern Russia makes it the ideal location for spa towns and seaside resorts.

Education

Universal, free education, and near universal literacy, are positive legacies of the Soviet era. However, the educational system was different from that in western Europe and is now changing to provide a broader curriculum rather than more narrow specialization.

Primary and secondary education in Russia is still almost entirely state-run. Since the end of the Soviet system in 1991, private education has been permitted but, by 2008, fewer than 1 percent of students attended private schools. At university level, however, around 17 percent of students attend private institutions.

PRESCHOOL EDUCATION

Since the Soviet era, when it became normal for both parents to work, preschool education has been widely funded by the state and provided by regional and local governments. In Soviet times, this provision amounted to little more than child care from age one through three, although kindergarten education was provided from age three to age seven. This system ended with the collapse of the Soviet Union, and many nursery and kindergarten buildings were sold.

Early in the twenty-first century, kindergarten education is generally provided for Russian children from age five, although, in some cities, there are not enough places for all children, and there is a waiting list. More than 80 percent of preschool-age children are enrolled in some form of education, the majority in kindergartens. Although participation in preschool is the norm among the urban population, fewer than one-half of children in rural areas attend kindergartens or similar institutions. In Soviet times, kindergarten education was free, but charges were introduced in 2004; after widespread public protests, charges were limited to a maximum of one-fifth of the costs. Exemptions are made for twins, the children of refugees and students, and other social groups. In modern times, a small minority of preschool children receive private education.

PRIMARY EDUCATION

Many children begin primary education at age seven having already learned the Russian alphabet, either at kindergarten or at home. In four years at primary school, students acquire basic skills in reading, writing, and math. Many students attend schools that offer the full 11-year course of education from age 7 through 18—the age of graduation was raised to 18 in 2007. At age 11, students begin secondary education; in rural areas, students typically transfer to a school in a town or city. It is common for one teacher to teach a class throughout their four-year primary schooling, except for specialized subjects such as foreign languages (which are not always available) and physical education. In modern times, a small but growing number of children are not enrolled in school.

SECONDARY EDUCATION

At age 11, students begin the middle-school element of secondary education, which lasts for four years. Russian is compulsory throughout, but local languages may also be taught. The normal curriculum comprises Russian language, one or two foreign languages (usually English, French, or German), physics, math, Russian and world history, geography, and Russian literature. The curriculum is fixed, and students have no choice of options. After successfully completing ninth grade (after the first four years of secondary education), students obtain a certificate of secondary education. They can then either continue their education at the same school or move to a technical school. There is also the option to leave school, but the student's parents and the local authority must both consent.

A 1949 Russian stamp celebrating child care, which was free during the Soviet era, as both parents were expected to work.

The Trans-Siberian Railroad terminus in Vladivostok.

ECONOMIC CHALLENGES

The transition from a centrally planned economy to a free market system was the primary challenge for Russia after 1991. In the early 1990s, necessary economic reforms, such as price liberalization and privatization, were carried out. Unfortunately, the government opted for sudden "shock" market methods—radical measures that damaged the Russian economy and society, bringing hyperinflation, mass unemployment, and the conditions that encouraged the elements of "wild capitalism": corruption, racketeering, and crime.

Because of these shock reforms, Russia was suddenly opened to world market competition. The better quality and low prices of the vast majority of imported goods depressed internal industrial and food production, which could not compete. At the same time, the reforms relied on foreign aid and large-scale foreign investments in the economy, which quickly collapsed. As a result, in the 1990s, Russia's GDP (gross domestic product, the total value of all the goods and services produced in a country in a fixed term, usually one year) contracted by some 40 percent. Consequently, the everyday lives of the majority (around 80 percent of the population) became much more difficult, and poverty increased.

By 1998, the economy faced a severe crisis. A financial crisis began on August 17, 1998, wiping away the economic achievement of the new Russia. The national currency, the ruble, fell precipitously; the government admitted bankruptcy and defaulted on payment of $40 billion in ruble bonds, and industrial output dropped. However, many key institutions of a market economy had been created. State-owned corporations and factories had been sold to private companies or individuals; millions of people became owners of their flats and houses.

After 1998, Russian GDP growth restarted; Russian enterprises managed to work in market conditions, and managers acquired skills to react to market signals. The nation was able to recover from the August 1998 financial crisis because of cheap exports (the Russian currency, the ruble, was low in value) and by exporting oil.

After 2000, Russia maintained industrial output, with (until mid-2008) an annual 7 percent growth in GDP, substantial growth in real personal consumption, high rates of construction, and considerable retail and investment activity. By 2007, Russia had achieved steady economic expansion, increased output, attained double-digit personal income growth and real personal consumption growth, as well as a significant decrease in unemployment. The nation had foreign-currency reserves of nearly $480 billion (then the third-largest in the world) and a $144 billion stabilization fund from surplus oil and gas revenue. However, a major world downturn in late 2008 and other problems created many economic challenges.

A weakening world economy in 2008 and 2009 decreased demand for primary commodities, upon which Russian economic growth depends. Some 80 percent of Russia's exports are oil, natural gas, metals, and timber, and overreliance upon these few sectors makes the Russian economy vulnerable to changes in demand and changes in world prices for these commodities. This downturn had also reduced public revenues and decreased the amount available to spend on social security, culture, education, and health care. Russia's new wealth is very unevenly distributed, and while there is a small class made wealthy through the privatization of state-owned companies after 1991, many people still live in poverty. This is particularly true of older people, whose pensions are meager.

The stability of the Russian economy is also perceived to be threatened by increasing state intervention and restrictions on liberty. Under Vladimir Putin (born 1952; in office as president 1999–2008 and as prime minister from 2008), state control increased, discouraging foreign investment. Many investors, both domestic and foreign, have also been discouraged by Russia's long-standing problems with infrastructure, widespread corruption among officials, endemic organized crime, and socioeconomic networks that run the economy in a non-Western style. Early in the twenty-first century, high global energy prices attracted foreign investment to Russia, despite the threat of government takeovers of petroleum industries as state intervention increased under Putin. Reforms are still urgently needed, strengthening property rights in Russia and liberalizing

state control over the economy to convince foreign investors that the move toward an open, free market economy is permanent and secure.

Crime, particularly white-collar or economic crime, is a major challenge. Especially in services, there is a large informal or gray economy that is unregulated and untaxed, and the consequent loss of revenue is a concern to the authorities. While racketeering and criminal activities received much international publicity in the 1990s, by the middle of the first decade of the twenty-first century, the Russian authorities had been successful in countering much criminal economic activity. However, corruption remains a problem, with many officials and business people expecting bribes; the volume of corruption in the country was estimated at $316 billion in 2005. The principal causes of this growing problem are weakened controls over authorities since the collapse of Communism and the increased greed of officials.

In the 1990s, many factories, companies, and resources were sold to politically connected people and private companies. Since then, the authorities have taken action against individuals whom they consider too politically powerful. Today, state-run companies with substantial financial resources are a strong economic force again. Some are famous not only in Russia, but worldwide, for example: Gazprom, the national gas company; Rosneft, the national oil company; Aeroflot, the national airline;

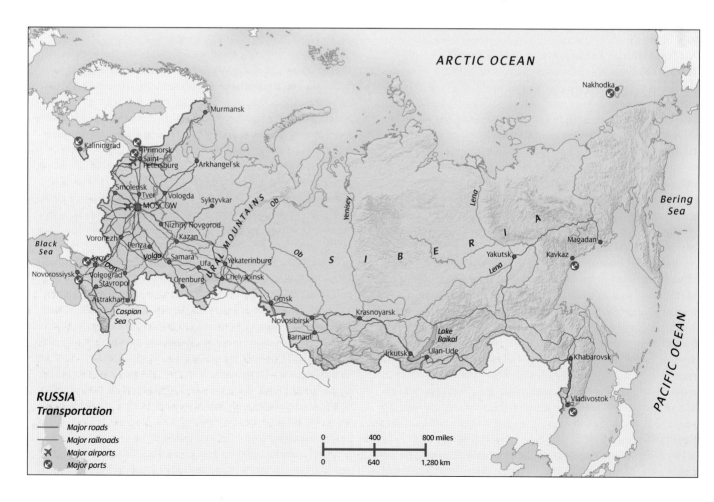

RUSSIA
Transportation

— Major roads
— Major railroads
✕ Major airports
⊗ Major ports

The Krasnoyarsk hydroelectric dam on the Yenisey River in Siberia.

Rosoboronexport, the defense-export state corporation; Sberbank, the savings bank; and Gazprombank, the commercial bank. High-ranking government officials serve, or have served, as chairs of these companies. In this way, government now plays a dominant role in the economy once again. The share of large companies controlled by the state is growing, and small and medium-sized businesses contribute less than 15 percent to the Russian GDP.

The Russian economy is increasingly controlled by large enterprises. These corporations, state-owned or private, often dominate local or regional economies and control the whole production cycle. Such enterprises in modern Russia are normally profitable. However, there are also many enterprises that make no profit.

On the ground, the Russian economy is a patchwork of developed and less-developed areas. The largest and most highly developed regions of the Russian Federation are the central region, based in Moscow and Saint Petersburg; the mid-Volga area, which is centered on the cities of Kazan, Nizhny Novgorod, and Samara; the Urals region, centered on Yekaterinburg; southern Siberia, centered on Novosibirsk; and the Russian Far East, which is centered on the cities of Khabarovsk and Vladivostok. These centers are distinguished by the heaviest concentrations of population, industrial sites, services, and culture. Some other industrial centers, such as Rostov-na-Donu and Volgograd, also stand out. General economic growth depends upon the potential of these developed regions and cities as regional growth poles to spread prosperity to neighboring territories and remote locations in Russia. Recent progress in administrative reform and intergovernmental fiscal relations may enhance this progress.

NATURAL RESOURCES

Natural resources in the Russian Federation include the world's largest reserves of coal, nearly one-third of the world's forests, fertile soils, and major reserves of oil and natural gas, manganese, gold, potash, bauxite, nickel, lead, zinc, and copper, as well as plentiful sites for hydroelectric power installations. The country is self-sufficient in energy.

Oil and natural gas come from enormous fields in the northern regions of western Siberia, from the Volga-Urals region, and the Komi field, in the north. These fields are linked to the major cities and their industries by an extensive pipeline network that connects with other networks across Europe, to which oil and natural gas are exported.

The oil-gas industry is a key sector of the Russian economy, and, from 1999 through 2007, the share of oil and natural gas in Russia's GDP has increased from 12.7 percent to 31.6

percent. As a result of higher revenues from rising oil prices, Russia has been able to bring the national debt down to acceptable levels, and high energy prices have greatly improved Russia's finances, primarily the federal budget, due to higher tax revenues. Today, the state-run natural gas monopoly, Gazprom, is the world's largest gas producer and exporter, with enormous reserves at its disposal. It supplies around one-quarter of Europe's gas needs, giving Russia political leverage in Europe. Russia is also one of the world's largest oil exporters. The Russian government repurchased a controlling share of Gazprom (50.002 percent) and tightened its control over the entire oil and gas sector by confiscating certain facilities and plants and strengthening rules to ensure that the industry pays its taxes regularly.

Much of Russia's power sector is still based on coal, and the nation has vast coalfields. The largest are in southern Siberia, close to the line of the Trans-Siberian Railroad. The greatest amount comes from the Kuznetsk Basin, which alone produces more than 40 percent of Russia's coal. Other fields in southern Siberia contribute another 35 percent. There are, however, larger coalfields in northern Siberia, in the Lena and Tunguska basins,

Nearly one-third of the world's forests are in Russia, but only around half of this area is commercially accessible and less than 10 percent is exploited.

but, because these fields are in regions with a harsh climate, they are mostly unexploited. There are other coalfields in the Russian part of the Donets Basin, adjoining Ukraine, and in Arctic northern European Russia. The greater part of the Russian coal industry is privatized, but many unprofitable mines, which had relied upon state subsidies, have closed.

Large hydroelectric power stations have been constructed on dams across the Volga, Ob, Angara, Yenisey, and Kama rivers. The course of the Volga River, in particular, has been altered by the creation of reservoirs. Many waterways that have not yet been harnessed to produce hydropower await similar exploitation.

Other natural resources include iron, which is found in large reserves at Kursk (in European Russia), in the Urals, the Kola Peninsula, and at several locations in Siberia. Major iron and steel facilities have been constructed close to some of these deposits. Nonferrous metals and precious and semiprecious stones are found in many locations spread across the country.

AGRICULTURE

Under Communism, the land was taken into state ownership and, in modern times, the collectives and state farms of the Soviet era still largely exist, although they are now mostly run as cooperatives. Little land has been privatized, and much of that is

of poor quality. Although the right to own and farm land privately has been introduced, little agricultural production comes from the private sector. Despite mechanization and the world's largest fertilizer industry, Russian crop yields are low compared with other major producers. The farming sector also experiences occasional poor harvests and has generally inadequate storage and transportation facilities.

There are significant regional differences in agriculture depending upon climate, terrain, and soil type. The Central Black Earth region of European Russia is a major cereal-growing area, producing wheat and barley. Warmer southern areas grow corn, fruits, and, in some places, grapes for wine. More marginal areas concentrate upon potatoes, vegetables, and fodder crops, while in the north and across much of Siberia little or no agriculture is possible. The harsh climate and difficult terrain restrict farming to less than 15 percent of the national area, with arable farming limited to some 7.2 percent. Major Russian crops include wheat, barley, oats, sugar beets, sunflowers (for seeds), potatoes, vegetables, and fruit. Large numbers of cattle, sheep, and poultry are raised. In modern times, farming (together with forestry and fishing) employs 10.8 percent of the workforce and supplies 4.7 percent of Russia's GDP.

Russia has traditionally had problems providing enough food for its needs, and this is, in part, a matter of organization, distances, and distribution. The processes of manufacturing agricultural raw materials to supply and distribute food have not always been smooth. This is influenced by the vast distances involved within the country, the largest in area in the world, and by the restriction of agriculture to relatively few areas. People in some parts of Russia must rely upon food that is transported hundreds of miles. Since the end of state regulation and the introduction of (limited) privatization since 1991, progress in agriculture has been extremely slow, and much of the industry still relies upon state subsidies.

Forestry makes a major contribution to the Russian economy. In the taiga belt across the northern part of both European and Asiatic Russia, and in the mixed forest zone to the south, Russia contains one of the world's largest reserves of timber. More than 40 percent of the nation is covered by trees, with conifers dominating. Russia's forests, directly and indirectly, employ nearly one million people in logging, paper, wood pulp, cardboard, furniture, and woodworking industries, and the nation produces about 20 percent of the world's softwood. In modern times, there are concerns about overexploitation of resources and, although the authorities publicly advocate sustainable forestry, the industry, which is state-owned, continues deforestation at a faster rate than replacement.

The Russian fishing industry is one of the four largest in the world, with trawler fleets fishing both the Atlantic and Pacific oceans. The fleet includes many factory ships that can sail far from Russian ports and can process fish at sea. The main fishing ports in the west are Saint Petersburg and Kaliningrad along the Baltic coast and Murmansk and Arkhangel'sk along the Arctic Ocean coast. In the east, the main port is Vladivostok. Fishing is also

A metal casting plant for the Kamaz heavy-duty truck manufacturer in Naberezhnye Chelny, Tatarstan.

practiced on inland waterways, including the Caspian Sea, where sturgeon are caught for their roe (caviar). The main catches of the Russian fishing industry are pollack, salmon, herring, and cod, although catches of cod are now greatly reduced.

INDUSTRY

Russia is a leading industrial power producing oil products, metals, construction materials, chemicals (including fertilizers and pharmaceuticals), machines and machine tools, construction

STANDARD OF LIVING

In 2007, GDP per capita in the Russian Federation was $14,800, adjusted for purchasing power parity (PPP), a formula that allows comparison between living standards in different countries. In 2007, some 15.8 percent of Russians lived in poverty, with poverty concentrated among older people, particularly the retired, and in rural areas.

EMPLOYMENT IN RUSSIA

Sector	Percentage of labor force
Agriculture and forestry	10.8 percent
Industry	28.8 percent
Services	60.4 percent

Source: Russian government, 2007

In 2007, 6.2 percent of the labor force was unemployed; many people are underemployed.

RUSSIA'S GDP

The gross domestic product (GDP) of Russia was $2.09 trillion in 2007. This figure is adjusted for purchasing power parity (PPP), an exchange rate at which goods in one country cost the same as goods in another.

MAIN CONTRIBUTORS TO THE RUSSIAN GDP

Agriculture, forestry, and fishing	4.7 percent
Industry	39.1 percent
Services	56.2 percent

Source: CIA, 2007

materials, automobiles, tractors, railroad transportation equipment, agricultural machinery, textiles, consumer goods and other items for domestic consumption, aircraft and space vehicles, medical and scientific instruments, electric power–generating equipment, and defense equipment.

The machine-building industry is a major sector of Russian industry. Its products include turbines and boilers; generators; machine tools; parts and components for the aircraft, agricultural vehicle, automobile, and railroad industries; and armaments, including rockets and tanks. Many of these industries are concentrated in a small number of cities. The automobile industry, for example, is concentrated at Nizhny Novgorod, Tol'yatti (where cars are constructed under license to Fiat, the Italian car manufacturer), Saint Petersburg, Izhevsk, and Moscow, while the aerospace industry is centered in Moscow and Irkutsk.

The chemical industry relies upon Russian coal, oil, and natural gas, as well as mineral salts and other natural resources, as its raw materials. The industry includes large fertilizer facilities, many of which are situated in the Central Black Earth agricultural region, where the fertilizers are used. The nation's other major industries include the textile and clothing sector, which is largely centered in the main cities of European Russia, where a number of towns that specialize in cotton and artificial textiles lie east of Moscow, and consumer goods industries, the largest of which are centered in Moscow and Saint Petersburg.

The most successful modern Russian industries are characterized by high performance and international reputation, for example, armaments, watches, and aircraft. These and other manufactured products are highly competitive in world markets. Russian industry appears highly diverse, but the range of products is not large in an economy that once put quantity before quality, and, in some cases, the Russian industrial sector faces challenges in design and in updating machinery and production methods. Types of manufactured exports are relatively limited (compared with the size of the economy), although the numbers exported are impressive. As a result, Russian industry still requires further modernization and diversification.

SERVICES

Under Communism, the service sector was not as highly developed as those of Western economies. Since the collapse of the Soviet Union, the banking sector has diversified and expanded but, during the transition to a free market, many new banks became insolvent. Today, Russia has a large number of commercial banks, many of which are state-owned. There are also considerable numbers of foreign banks operating in Russia. The Russian Central Bank regulates the nation's financial system.

A construction boom has been accompanied by an expansion in real estate; the insurance and financial sectors have also grown. New shops and modern shopping malls have been built in the twenty-first century, and the retail sector, which was once characterized as limited and unexciting, has developed. There are also many new hotels and restaurants, some of which cater to tourists. Foreign tourism has developed, with the greatest numbers attracted to Saint Petersburg.

Many people employed in the service sector work for the national or local governments in defense, administration, education, health care, and other public sectors. However, public sector services are, compared with private industry, poorly rewarded, and many workers have left the public sector.

TRADE

In 2007, Russia exported goods and services worth $355.5 billion while importing goods and services valued at $223.4 billion. Consequently, the nation has a large trade surplus. These favorable terms of trade are mainly the result of exporting oil and natural gas to Europe. Russia's international trade is fast growing, although the global economic downturn that started in 2008 has led to a contraction. In 2007, the nation's principal exports were petroleum and petroleum products, natural gas, wood and wood products (including paper), metals, chemicals, and manufactures (including machinery, machine tools, and defense equipment and armaments). Compared with the Soviet era, during which a large share of Russian exports was machinery, Russia now exports far fewer machines and more oil and natural gas.

Russian external trade now relies heavily on commodities, especially oil and gas, which account for more than one-half of Russia's federal tax receipts. Russia is the world's largest exporter of natural gas and the second-largest oil exporter. The principal recipients of exports from Russia in 2007 were the Netherlands (which took 12 percent of Russian exports), Italy (8 percent), Germany (8 percent), Turkey (5 percent), Belarus (5 percent), Ukraine (5 percent), China including Hong Kong, Switzerland, Poland, and Kazakhstan.

The main imports into Russia are machinery and transportation equipment, consumer goods, medicines, meat, sugar, other foods and beverages, and semifinished metal products. The principal suppliers of these imports to Russia in 2007 were Germany (which supplied 13 percent of Russia's imports), China including Hong Kong (12 percent), Ukraine (7 percent), Japan (6 percent), the United States (5 percent), Belarus, South Korea, Italy, France, Kazakhstan, and Finland.

Since 1991, Russia has developed closer trading relations with countries of the European Union (EU), although trade links with other former Soviet republics in Central Asia and the Caucasus as well as in eastern Europe have been retained, but often not on such a large scale. The former Soviet republics, including Russia itself, are trying to find their own niche in the global marketplace. The Russian government has continued to promote trade efforts by removing most of the remaining barriers to international trade, which had been established to protect local producers. Negotiations to join the World Trade Organization (WTO) have been completed, but some doubts remain concerning WTO membership. Russia is not fully ready to meet WTO standards, and there remain some serious problems regarding agriculture, the domestic automobile industry, and banking.

TRANSPORTATION AND COMMUNICATION

Russia's transportation networks connect people, resources, and industry across vast distances. The nation stretches from the Baltic Sea to the Pacific Ocean, and the distances are so large

Western Siberia's oil reserves have been exploited since the 1970s; the area now supplies two-thirds of Russian oil.

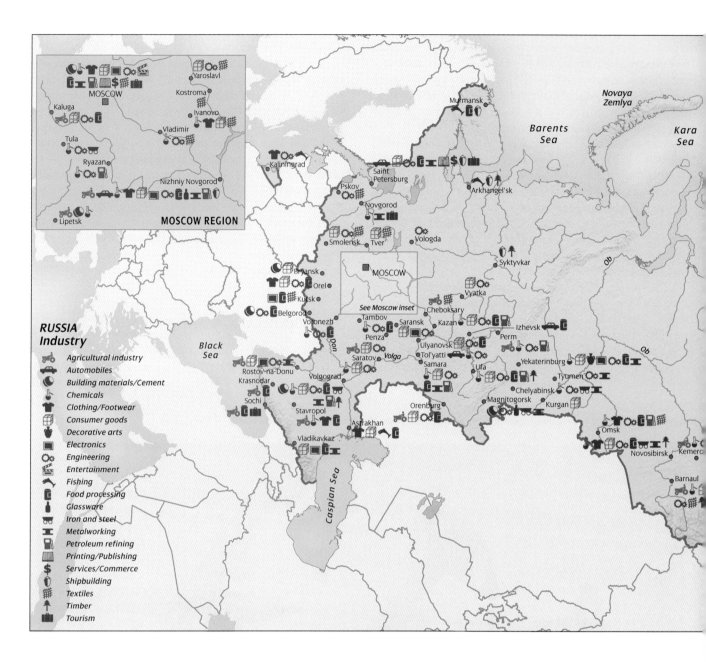

RUSSIA
Industry

Agricultural industry
Automobiles
Building materials/Cement
Chemicals
Clothing/Footwear
Consumer goods
Decorative arts
Electronics
Engineering
Entertainment
Fishing
Food processing
Glassware
Iron and steel
Metalworking
Petroleum refining
Printing/Publishing
Services/Commerce
Shipbuilding
Textiles
Timber
Tourism

that railroads rather than roads are the most important mode of transportation, carrying more than 80 percent of the nation's freight. There are some 66,584 miles (107,157 km) of railroads, including around 18,641 miles (some 30,000 km) of industrial and mining lines.

The railway sector has been substantially reformed but remains in public ownership under a single company. Russian railroads transport millions of passengers annually and connect all the major towns and cities in the country. The most famous line is the Trans-Siberian Railroad, which links Moscow with Vladivostok in a seven-day journey. The larger cities have commuter railroads catering to city workers, and Moscow, Saint Petersburg, Kazan, Yekaterinburg, Nizhny Novgorod, Novosibirsk, and Samara have subways.

The Russian highway system covers 579,863 miles (933,000 km), of which some 18,640 miles (30,000 km) are

expressways and 450,484 miles (724,984 km) are other paved roads. There are 110,614 miles (178,016 km) of unpaved roads, some of which are impassable in winter, owing to snow, or in spring, because of meltwater. Car ownership has greatly increased in Russia since 1991 but is, as yet, nowhere near western European levels. Road user charges are insufficient to cover costs, and the road system is poorly maintained. The network is also inadequate, with notable gaps in the system; there is not, for example, a direct road link between Tatarstan and the neighboring city of Samara.

Water transportation has been important in the past but, since the third quarter of the twentieth century, this sector's roles have been diminishing. Russia's primary transportation routes are east-west, as well as radial routes from the largest cities. However, Russia's navigable waterways run north-south. At the dissolution of the Soviet Union, Russia lost warm-water

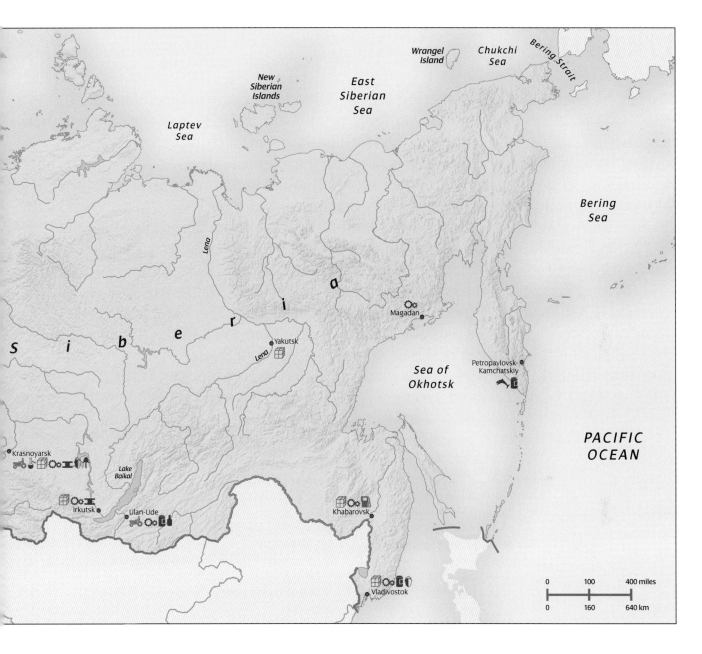

ports, and some of the main ports left within the Russian Federation freeze in winter. Some ports, such as Murmansk and Arkhangel'sk along the Arctic Ocean coast and, in the east, Vladivostok, along the Pacific Ocean coast, are remote from the main centers of Russian industry. The main Russian ports are now Saint Petersburg (which freezes in winter), Kaliningrad, Azov, and Novorossiysk.

Russia has 601 airports with paved runways but only 15 that serve international flights. This small number is a relic of Communist times, when access to the Soviet Union was strictly controlled. The principal international airports are the three main airports in Moscow and Saint Petersburg airport. Despite the vast distances within Russia, domestic internal aviation is not nearly as developed as might be expected. This is, in large part, due to the relatively high cost of flights compared with average incomes. Many regional airports require substantial repairs and modernization, as does much of the railroad system and, particularly, the roads of Russia.

In 1991, Russia's telecommunications system was out of date, and many people were on a waiting list for connection. Substantial improvements to the nation's telecommunications network have been made, and digital communications now link the major cities. There are now more than one thousand companies offering communications services in Russia. In 2006, there were nearly 44 million main telephone lines in the Russian Federation, and more than 170 million mobile cellular phones were registered in 2007 (compared with only one million in 1998), that is, considerably more than the country's population. This figure in part reflects the perceived unreliability, or unavailability, of the fixed-line service in some parts of the country. In 2007, some 30 million Russians had Internet access.

R. V. KASHBRASIEV

Ukraine

The largest country in area entirely in Europe, Ukraine became independent when the Soviet Union collapsed (1991). Kievan Rus, the area around Kiev, was the cradle of the first Russian state and flourished in the tenth and eleventh centuries, before being toppled by a Tatar invasion from the east in the thirteenth century. Most of what is now Ukraine was subsequently incorporated into Lithuania, but some coastal regions were (at least nominally) subject to the Turkish Ottoman Empire. In 1667, the area east of the Dnieper River was ceded to Russia by Poland-Lithuania. In the partitions of Poland (1772, 1793, and 1795), Austria gained what is now western Ukraine, while Russia gained the rest of the Ukrainian lands that had been part of Poland-Lithuania. After the 1917 Russian Revolution, a Ukrainian republic was declared, but Poland annexed the west and Russian armies retook the center and east in 1919. The Ukrainian Soviet Socialist Republic (SSR) was part of the Soviet Union from 1922 through 1991. Ukraine, once called the "bread basket of the Soviet Union," suffered famine in the 1930s and, from 1941 through 1944, was occupied by German forces during World War II (1939–1945). Ukraine declared sovereignty in 1990 and became independent in 1991.

GEOGRAPHY

Location	Eastern Europe, between the Black Sea and the Russian Federation
Climate	Mediterranean with mild, rainy winters and warm, dry summers in southern Crimea; temperate in western Ukraine; continental with cold, snowy winters and warm summers in the east and north
Area	233,090 sq. miles (603,700 sq. km)
Coastline	1,729 miles (2,782 km)
Highest point	Hoverla 6,762 feet (2,061 m)
Lowest point	Black Sea 0 feet
Terrain	Mainly fertile plains (steppes) and plateaus; mountains in the far west (the Carparthians) and in the Crimean Peninsula
Natural resources	Coal, iron ore, lignite, building materials, oil, natural gas, hydroelectric power potential, nickel, manganese, timber
Land use	
Arable land	53.8 percent
Permanent crops	1.5 percent
Other	44.7 percent
Major rivers	Dnieper, Dniester, Donets
Major lakes	Kremenchuk-Oskol reservoir, Kakhovka reservoir, Kiev reservoir
Natural hazards	Floods

METROPOLITAN AREAS, 2007 POPULATION

Urban population	68 percent
Kiev	2,810,000
Kiev City	2,660,000
Kharkiv (formerly Kharkov)	1,840,000
Kharkiv City	1,465,000
Dnipropetrovs'k (formerly Dnepropetrovsk)	1,480,000
Dnipropetrovs'k City	1,056,000
Dniprodzerzhysk (formerly Dneprodzerzhinsk)	250,000
Donetsk	1,440,000
Donetsk City	1,000,000
Makiyivka (formerly Makeyevka)	376,000
Odesa (formerly Odessa)	1,065,000
Odesa City	1,007,000
Zaporizhzhya (formerly Zaporozhye)	799,000
Lviv (formerly Lvov)	734,000
Kryvyj Rih (formerly Krivoyrog)	697,000
Kramatorsk	530,000
Kramatorsk City	175,000
Mykolayiv (formerly Nikolayev)	509,000
Mariupol	482,000
Luhansk	453,000
Horlivka (formerly Gorlovka)	380,000
Horlivka City	279,000
Vinnytsya (formerly Vinnitsa)	360,000
Simferopol	342,000
Sevastopol	340,000
Kherson	319,000
Poltava	310,000

Chernihiv (formerly Chernigov)	300,000
Cherkassy	293,000
Sumy	282,000
Zhytomyr (formerly Zhitomir)	278,000
Alchevsk	253,000
Alchevsk City	117,000

Source: Ukrainian government estimates, 2005

NEIGHBORS AND LENGTH OF BORDERS

Belarus	554 miles (891 km)
Hungary	64 miles (103 km)
Moldova*	584 miles (940 km)
Poland	266 miles (428 km)
Romania	334 miles (538 km)
Russian Federation	979 miles (1,576 km)
Slovakia	56 miles (90 km)

* Includes the border with the internationally unrecognized Transnistria Republic.

FLAG

The flag of Ukraine comprises two horizontal bands, pale blue over gold. The colors are those of ancient Kievan Rus (nine centuries ago); in modern times, blue is said to symbolize the sky, mountains, and waterways, while gold represents fields of cereal crops. The design became the national flag of Ukraine in 1992.

POPULATION

Population	46,560,000 (2007 government estimate)
Population density	200 per sq. mile (77 per sq. km)
Population growth	-0.7 percent a year
Birthrate	9.6 births per 1,000 of the population
Death rate	15.9 deaths per 1,000 of the population
Population under age 15	13.9 percent
Population over age 65	16.1 percent
Sex ratio	106 males for 100 females
Fertility rate	1.3 children per woman
Infant mortality rate	9.2 deaths per 1,000 live births
Life expectancy at birth	
Total population	68.1 years
Female	74.2 years
Male	62.2 years

ECONOMY

Currency	Hryvnia (UAH)
Exchange rate (2008)	$1 = UAH 6.11
Gross domestic product (2007)	$324.8 billion
GDP per capita (2007)	$7,000
Unemployment rate (2007)	2.3 percent (official); most Western estimates are around 7 percent
Population under poverty line (2003)	37.7 percent
Exports	$49.8 billion (2007 CIA estimate)
Imports	$60.4 billion (2007 CIA estimate)

GOVERNMENT

Official country name	Ukraine
Conventional short form	Ukraine
Former name	Ukrainian Soviet Socialist Republic

Nationality	
noun	Ukrainian
adjective	Ukrainian
Official language	Ukrainian
Capital city	Kiev
Type of government	Semipresidential republic; democracy
Voting rights	18 years, universal
National anthem	"Shche ne vmerla Ukraina" (Ukraine's glory has not perished)
National day	Independence Day, August 24 (1991; from the Soviet Union)

TRANSPORTATION

Railroads	13,964 miles (22,473 km)
Highways	105,274 miles (169,422 km)
Paved roads	102,906 miles (165,611 km)
Unpaved roads	2,368 miles (3,811 km)
Navigable waterways	1,400 miles (2,253 km); (most on the Dnieper River)
Airports	
International airports	10
Paved runways	193

POPULATION PROFILE, 2007 ESTIMATES

Ethnic groups	
Europeans	virtually 100 percent (of which Ukrainians form 78 percent; Russians 17 percent; Belarussians, Moldovans, Bulgarians, Tatars, Hungarians, Poles, and other Europeans almost 5 percent)

Religions	
Ukrainian Orthodox, Kiev Patriarchate	15 percent
Ukrainian Orthodox, Moscow Patriarchate	8 percent
Ukrainian Autocephalous Orthodox	2 percent
Ukrainian Greek Catholic	8 percent
Roman Catholic	2 percent
Various Protestant Churches	2 percent
Jewish	1 percent
Others	3 percent
Various nonpracticing Orthodox Christians	21 percent
Nonreligious	38 percent

Languages	
Ukrainian	67 percent as a first language
Russian	24 percent as a first language, but understood by the majority
Belarussian, Romanian, Bulgarian, Hungarian, Polish, and other European languages	9 percent

Adult literacy	over 99 percent

A view over Lviv, one of the main cultural centers of Ukraine.

A Ukrainian folk dance group, dressed in traditional costume.

ages and now has the appearance of a seventeenth-century Ukrainian baroque building. Another religious center of Kievan Rus is the Kiev Pechersk Lavra (the Monastery of the Caves): it consists of caves, bell towers, monuments, and churches that also underwent renovations in the seventeenth century, and their present exterior appearance is of the Ukrainian baroque style.

Once an independent principality and later a center of Russian governors, Chernihiv (formerly Chernigov) is an important center of Ukrainian architecture. Chernihev is home to the five-domed Savior Cathedral (built around 1030 and the oldest in Ukraine), Saint Catherine's Church, and the Uspensky (Dormition) and Troitsky (Trinity) monasteries. Kozelets Abbey in Chernihiv is a fine example of Ukrainian baroque, also known as Cossack baroque, which is usually thought of as being Ukraine's national architecture. Ukrainian baroque differs from west and central European baroque in being simpler and less ornamented. This style is also characterized by onion-shaped domes, borrowed from Muscovite architecture.

As Russia gradually extended its rule into Ukraine, Russian-style buildings were erected in the region's cities. Saint Andrew's Church in Kiev, a mid-eighteenth century building, is a typical example of Russian imperial architecture in Ukraine. When Russia developed southern Ukrainian cities, such as Odesa, Kherson, and Sevastopol, entire downtown districts of Russian imperial buildings were constructed, for example the mid-nineteenth-century Potemkin Steps and surrounding buildings in Odesa.

Under Soviet rule, public buildings were planned on a monumental scale. Structures in the style that came to be known as Constructivism were prominent, particularly in the downtown area of Kharkiv, which was the first capital of Soviet Ukraine. Typical of these are the huge Gosprom building and Dzerzhinsky Square (now known as Freedom Square). World War II (1939–1945) brought large-scale destruction to Ukraine's cities, and many were reconstructed to include buildings in the Stalinist, or Soviet Social Realist, style. In modern times, major buildings in Ukraine are generally in the international high-rise style, such as skyscrapers erected in the early twenty-first century along Rybalskyi Peninsula in Kiev.

Rural domestic architecture in Ukraine follows several different traditions, depending on the materials available for construction. Before modern times, rural houses were typically compact and often single-story. In the Carpathian Mountains and the west, timber was used to construct houses, while, in other places, clay or bricks were commonly used. Many houses were thatched.

Ukrainians in western Ukraine, especially in villages, retained traditional dress and ornaments into the twentieth century. Some older women wear *plakhta* (shawls), *zapaska* (skirts), and *ochipok* (headscarfs). Unmarried girls decorated their long braided hair with flowers and ornaments.

MUSIC AND PERFORMING ARTS

Kiev and Lviv are the main centers of theater in Ukraine. Kiev's Shevchenko Opera and Ballet Theater, originally known as the Russian Opera House, was established in 1867. It is one of the finest opera and ballet performance venues in the former Soviet Union and one of 28 major theaters in Ukraine. The National

Borscht, the national dish of Ukraine, is a soup made with beets. It is common to many eastern and central European cultures.

Academic Drama Theater, in Kiev, stages plays by classical and modern Ukrainian and Western playwrights. There are also major centers for the arts in Kharkiv and Odesa.

Ukrainian folk music is popular in the country and among the Ukrainian diaspora (Ukrainians living abroad). Traditional Ukrainian folk music derives from the music of Kievan Rus. In the time of Polish and later Russian domination, Ukrainian bards (*kobzars*) sang ballads with the accompaniment of the *bandura* or *kobza*, the national stringed instrument. The shepherds of the Carpathian Mountains in western Ukraine are famous for a lively folk style and for their traditional alpen horn (*trembita*).

Derived from early ritual dances, Ukrainian folk dance developed in two main traditions. Among Cossacks of the Dnieper region in the seventeenth and eighteenth centuries, dances such as the *hopak* and the *kasachok* were enjoyed. Among Ukrainians in the Carpathians in western Ukraine, the *hutsulka* and *kolomiyka* dances were developed. Later, under Polish influence, local variants of the polka and quadrille evolved in Ukraine. Peasant communities also preserved thematic dances such as the *kosari* (reapers) and *kovali* (blacksmiths). In modern times, Ukraine's dance heritage is preserved and popularized by companies such as Hryhory Veryovka Ukrainian Choir and Dance Ensemble and the Ukrainian State Song and Dance Ensemble, which are supported by the state. The principal Russian influence upon dance in Ukraine was the introduction of ballet and, in modern times, leading Ukrainian cities have prestigious ballet companies.

In classical music, the Ukrainian national school of music was pioneered by composer and pianist Mykola Lysenko (1842–1912), who is widely considered the father of Ukrainian classical music. Priest Mykola Leontovych (1877–1921) is best-

known for his arrangement of "Shchedryk," an ancient New Year's chant, which is known abroad as "Carol of the Bells," a popular short choral work. Like "Shchedryk," many Ukrainian pieces are derived in part from folk music.

Some pop music in Ukraine also draws inspiration from folk music, although Western pop music entered Ukraine from the 1960s. In the following decade, folk rock groups, such as Kobza, formed; since independence, a distinctly Ukrainian pop-folk genre has emerged. The most prominent artists include Ruslana (Ruslana Lyzhychko; born 1973), rock bands Okean Elzy and Vopli Vidopliassova, Sofia Rotaru (born 1947), and innovative folk singer Mariana Sadovska (born 1972).

FESTIVALS AND CEREMONIES

The first public holiday of the year in Ukraine is New Year's Day, followed by January 7, Orthodox Christmas Day. New Year is the main celebration of the year, marked in much the same way as Christmas in most of Europe. A tree, like a Christmas tree, is decorated; celebration meals and parties are held; and children receive presents and cakes. There is a second New Year celebration on January 14, according to the old Julian calendar—while civil society follows the Gregorian calendar, like most of the world, the Orthodox Church adheres to the Julian calendar, which is now 13 days different.

Other public holidays are International Women's Day (March 8); Orthodox Easter; Orthodox Whitsun; two days for Labor Day, on May 1 and 2; Victory Day on May 9, commemorating the end of World War II; Constitution Day (June 28); and the National Day, Independence Day, which is celebrated on August 24, the anniversary of the proclamation of independence in 1990 following the failed coup by Communist hardliners in Moscow, which effectively hastened the collapse of the Soviet Union. The birthday of Taras Schevchenko (March 9) is celebrated as the National Day of Ukrainian Poetry and Culture but is not a public holiday.

FOOD AND DRINK

Borscht, the national dish of Ukrainian cuisine, is cooked in a pot in the oven. The main ingredients for this rich, tasty soup include meat (beef or pork) boiled to make stock, *salo* (salted pig fat), beets, potatoes, tomatoes (fresh or pickled), carrots, and onions, fried before being put into the stock. Ukrainian borscht is often served with *galushki* (dumplings of home-made pasta covered in garlic sauce). Other favorite dishes are boiled dumplings with potatoes, cherries, cottage cheese (*vareniki*), and cabbage rolls with ground meat and rice (*holubtsi*). *Horilka*, or Ukrainian vodka, is considered the national drink.

I. KOTIN

DAILY LIFE

Ukrainian society is shaped by two cultures, ethnic Ukrainian and Russian, as well as by nearly seven decades of Soviet Communist rule. Since independence in 1991, Ukraine has been more open to Western influences.

Some 78 percent of the population of Ukraine are ethnically Ukrainian, although only 67 percent speak Ukrainian as a first language. About 17 percent of the population are ethnically Russian, but 24 percent speak Russian as a first language. The Russian language is almost universally understood in Ukraine. The remainder of the population are Belarussians (also given as Belarusians), Moldovans, Bulgarians, Tatars, Hungarians, Poles, and other Europeans. The ethnic and linguistic divide is partly territorial, with ethnic Ukrainians and Ukrainian speakers being a majority in the west and center, and ethnic Russians and Russian speakers a majority in much of the industrial east and in Crimea.

RELIGION

Despite 70 years of Communist atheist policy, religion is important in Ukraine. However, as a result of anti-religious propaganda in the Soviet period, Ukrainian society is mostly secular in nature. Some 38 percent of the population is nonreligious. The majority of the remainder regard themselves as belonging to a particular church but may not practice religion or have any religious belief.

There are three different Orthodox churches: Ukrainian Orthodox (Kiev Patriarchate), which claims 15 percent of the population; Ukrainian Orthodox (Moscow Patriarchate), claiming 8 percent; and Ukrainian Autocephalous Orthodox, 2 percent. Various nonpracticing Orthodox Christians, who regard themselves as part of the Orthodox culture, but who have no link with any church, account for around 21 percent of the population. The other principal churches in Ukraine are: Ukrainian Greek Catholic (accounting for 8 percent), Roman Catholic (2 percent), and various Protestant Churches (2 percent). Jews form 1 percent of the population.

The division of Orthodoxy into different churches is both historic and recent. Orthodox Christianity was introduced to Ukraine at the end of the tenth century, and the major denominations in Ukraine all follow Byzantine rites. Following the Council of Brest of 1596, the Orthodox priests of present-day western Ukraine accepted the supremacy of the pope but were allowed to retain Orthodox rituals and Old Slavonic as the language of liturgy. The Ukrainian Greek Catholic Church is the heir of this decision. Technically, the followers of this church (known as the Uniates) are Catholics, but they are closer in practices to the Orthodox Church than to Roman Catholicism.

The prosecution of the Greek Catholic Church by Soviet dictator Joseph Stalin (1879–1953; leader of the Soviet Communist Party and effectively ruler of Russia 1922–1953) after 1946, accusing it of collaboration with the Nazis and with Ukrainian nationalists, led to the transfer of many Greek Catholic churches to the Russian Orthodox Church.

The Orthodox Church faced new problems in Ukraine with the collapse of the Soviet Union in 1991 and the proclamation of an independent Ukraine. The Orthodox Church was part of the Russian Church, and loyalty to the Moscow patriarchate was considered unpatriotic by many Ukrainian nationalists. Consequently, nationalist Ukrainian clergy, supported by the Ukrainian authorities, founded the separate Ukrainian Orthodox Church of the Kiev patriarchate as a national church. It did not, however, automatically receive all the churches and parishes of the former Ukrainian exarchate of the Russian Orthodox Church. Presently, more than one-half of the Orthodox parishes in Ukraine are controlled by the Ukrainian Orthodox (Moscow Patriarchate) Church. Also, a significant number of churches belong to another, smaller, secessionist organization known as the Autocephalous Orthodox Church. The two main Orthodox Churches are, in part, geographically identifiable, with Orthodox Christians loyal to the Kiev patriarchate (as well as Greek Catholics) mainly in western Ukraine and those loyal to the Moscow patriarchate in the east.

FAMILY AND SOCIETY

The religious divide between east and west reflects a wider watershed in the country. The very name of the country, Ukraine, means "borderland," a reminder of the early modern history of the country when there was a Polish Ukraine on the borderland of Poland and a Russian Ukraine along the Russian borders. For much of this period, the Dnieper River was the divide. The territories of the two Ukraines had much in common but also differed culturally and linguistically. In western Ukraine, Polish culture dominated for centuries, until the expropriation of lands of the Polish nobles after an unsuccessful revolt in 1830. Eastern Ukraine, by contrast, was dominated by Russia.

The linguistic duality divides Ukraine. The number of Russian schools for the Russian-speaking population is diminishing, and the number of books published in Russian is also decreasing. The requirement to know the Ukrainian language for government officers is generally regarded as

The curved style of these modern apartment buildings in Kiev contrasts with the stark utilitarianism of Soviet architecture that remains in older parts of the city.

reasonable, but the artificial introduction of old words into modern Ukrainian, replacing commonly used Russian words, hinders the attempts to learn it, even by Ukrainians whose first language is Ukrainian.

The linguistic watershed in Ukrainian society is reflected in an urban-rural divide. The majority of the Russian-speaking population live in industrialized urban areas. The Ukrainian-speaking heartland is the rural Western Ukraine, where 90 percent of the population live in large villages. The rural regions are also areas where traditional, large patriarchal families still dominate. In eastern and northern Ukraine, generally, smaller families live mostly in cities. The population of Ukraine is declining due to a low birthrate (9.6 births per 1,000 of the population in 2007) and emigration. There has also been immigration, mainly ethnic Ukrainians returning to Ukraine from other parts of the former Soviet Union as well as the return of Crimean Tatars from Central Asia, to where they were deported by Stalin in 1944, having been accused of collaboration with the Germans in World War II.

Since independence, the population has fallen by more than 8 percent. At the same time, the population is aging, and some small rural communities are inhabited largely by older people, the young having gone to the cities or abroad in search of employment. One baby in five is born out of marriage, a much lower figure than that of western European countries. Ukrainian women also tend to have children later than in many European states: only one mother in four is under age 20.

Since 1991, many changes have occurred in Ukrainian society. Previously, society rather than the individual was stressed. Now, a marked growth in individualism is reflected even in clothes; whereas people used to dress in restrained colors and fashions, it is now no longer so easy to identify Ukrainians by their appearance as, for example, industrial workers or office workers. Consumerism has also developed as choice and a range of differently priced goods became available.

THE ROLE OF WOMEN

Although equal rights are enshrined in law, traditional gender stereotypes are still commonly held in Ukraine. Relatively few women have achieved high office in politics, with the notable exception of Yulia Tymoshenko (born 1960; in office as prime minister 2005 and from 2007), or in senior management in commerce and industry. It is sometimes claimed that ethnic Ukrainian women have made greater progress toward gender equality than ethnic Russian women in Ukraine. This may reflect the ancient Ukrainian matriarchal tradition, symbolized by Berehynia, the pre-Christian goddess who was mother and guardian of the nation. Under Russian rule, Ukrainian women retained more personal freedom than Russian women, and the Russian practice of *domostroi*, by which Russian men dominated the household and exercised the right to physically punish their spouses, was never accepted in Ukraine.

HEALTH AND WELFARE

Ukraine still follows many of the former Soviet policies regarding the provision of health care and social security. However, maintaining the once comprehensive welfare system is difficult, owing to an aging population and inadequate funding. Ukraine has retained many of the state's obligations to the public, including free medical care, education, and social services. In reality, however, many of these services are ineffective, and wealthier Ukrainians now opt for private medicine and education.

The principal causes of death in Ukraine are heart disease, cancers, and respiratory diseases. Many people smoke, and a significant number of deaths are identified as smoking-related, particularly in men, some 57 percent of whom smoke. The rate of smoking among Ukrainian women is lower than the European average. The health problems of many Ukrainian men are also related to alcohol consumption. Women's health problems in Ukraine are often associated with reproductive health. Although contraception is available, a relatively high number of pregnancies are terminated, and abortion is sometimes regarded as a method of birth control. Ukraine is thought to have the highest incidence of HIV-AIDS in Europe, spread by intravenous drug use among the young. There has also been an increase in the incidence of tuberculosis. Ukraine still faces the legacy of the accident at the nuclear power facility at Chernobyl, near Kiev, in 1986. There is a high incidence of child thyroid cancer in the immediate area of Chernobyl, and some 3.2 million Ukrainians suffered health problems as a result of Chernobyl, with 90,000 permanently disabled.

Economic difficulties since independence brought an initial contraction in the economy. As a result, health care funding decreased, while, at the same time, life expectancy fell. The state maintains hospitals and medical centers, and there is an emphasis on prevention. Increased costs of drugs and equipment have reduced the availability of certain treatments and procedures, and the health care system is now generally perceived to be inefficient and of a low quality by European standards. Primary care is maintained by municipalities, while the regions maintain hospitals. The state-funded structure, basically unchanged since Soviet days,

Housing

Owing to the large-scale destruction of many of Ukraine's cities during World War II, many homes in the country are relatively modern, having been built since 1945. However, the typical apartment buildings of suburban Ukraine generally offer small, poor-quality accommodations. Much of the housing stock is rented, owned by municipalities, but this urban housing is more modern than most rural accommodations. In a 2000 survey, it was found that only 10 percent of Ukrainian rural dwellings had an indoor toilet and only 30 percent a bath or shower.

began to be reformed early in the twenty-first century. Free health care is, in theory, available to all, but in practice, patients who are hospitalized pay for medication and food. Unofficial payments are also often expected to enable a patient to receive earlier treatment.

Mandatory social insurance provides payments for disability and sickness as well as unemployment benefits. Employees must have paid contributions for two to five years, depending upon the nature of the benefit, to receive payment. The state also provides pensions for elderly people, with men with 25 years of contributions being able to claim a state pension at age 65 and women with 20 years of contributions at age 55.

EDUCATION

Ukrainian children begin free, compulsory education at age six, although many receive preschool or kindergarten education, and stay in school for 12 years. Although school education is divided into primary, middle, and senior sections, the overwhelming majority of students remain in the same school throughout. At age 15 and 17, students take tests that determine eligibility to enroll at a university. Some 70 percent of schools teach in Ukrainian, while 29 percent do so in Russian.

University education is either privately funded, in which case there is no entrance requirement, or state subsidized for students achieving the required grades in the tests. State scholarships, whose continuing level depends upon performance, are paid to students but are not sufficient to cover living expenses; subsidized housing is available.

The country has a number of famous universities. What is now called the Ivan Franko University of Lviv was originally founded in 1661 and is the oldest university in Ukraine. Kiev University, now named for writer Taras Shevchenko (1814–1861), is the largest in Ukraine. Unlike Ivan Franko University, Kiev and some others offer instruction both in Ukrainian and Russian, depending upon a student's choice. Most of the documentation, however, is in Ukrainian, and the trend is to replace Russian by Ukrainian when and where possible.

I. KOTIN

Lviv is the center of Catholicism in Ukraine, and there are three cathedrals of different traditions in the city: Roman Catholic, Greek Catholic, and Armenian Catholic. The silhouette at sunset of the spires and domes of two churches can be seen here.

Kiev

The largest city in Ukraine, Kiev became the national capital of independent Ukraine in 1991. Historically Kiev was the center of the first Russian state, Kievan Rus.

In 2007, the Kiev metropolitan area was home to a population of 2,810,000, while 2,660,000 people lived within the city limits. Kiev lies along the banks of the Dnieper River, with the historic city on an area of high bluffs overlooking the valley.

KIEV IN HISTORY

The city was founded in the sixth or seventh century CE and was conquered by the Varangians, a Slav-Viking people, in the ninth century CE. In the 880s CE, the ruler of Novgorod seized Kiev and established it as the capital of the first Slavic state, which came to be known as Kievan Rus. Kiev developed as a trading center, commanding routes along the Dnieper and waterways to the north. After the introduction of Christianity in 988 CE, it became a center of learning and, by the twelfth century, was one of the leading cities of Europe.

In the twelfth and thirteenth centuries, Kiev was invaded by nomadic peoples from the east and was destroyed by a Mongol army in 1238. In the fourteenth century, the area was annexed by Lithuania, which united with Poland in 1569. In the seventeenth century, local Cossacks, aided by the Tatars, revolted against Polish rule, and the Cossacks took Kiev. Poland was unable to reassert control in the region, and an agreement between Russia and the Cossacks brought the area under Russian rule. In 1667, an autonomous Cossack state, centered in Kiev, came under Russian protection. Although Russian rule ended along the eastern bank of the Dnieper, Kiev along the western bank was also Russian. In 1793, at the Second Partition of Poland, Russia also gained Ukraine along the western bank.

Through the nineteenth century, commerce and industry developed. The city's population grew from 30,000 at the beginning of the nineteenth century, to 71,000 by 1866, to 127,000 by 1890, 248,000 in 1897, and 447,000 in 1911. The export of grain and agricultural industries promoted rapid growth, and Kiev became a center for Ukrainian culture and nationalism.

After the Russian Revolution (1917), a revolt in Kiev brought a declaration of Ukrainian independence (1918), but the Soviet Red Army soon occupied the city. Between March 1918 and May 1920, Kiev was subsequently occupied by Germans, forces supporting Ukrainian independence, monarchist White Russian troops, the Soviet Red Army, the Polish army, and, finally, the Red Army again. Because of Kiev's support for Ukrainian nationalism, the Soviet authorities made Kharkov (now Kharkiv), which had a large Russian minority, the capital of Ukraine until 1934. Through the 1930s, engineering, chemical, and other industries were established. In September 1941, German forces occupied Kiev. The city's Jewish population was subsequently murdered, many in a ravine known as Babi Yar, and many other citizens were taken to labor camps. The city was liberated in November 1943.

THE MODERN CITY

In 1991, Kiev became the national capital of an independent Ukraine. The city has financial, commercial, retail, and service industries; it has four major universities and many other institutions of higher education. Large numbers of people are employed in administration, but the city also has a major industrial sector with engineering, metalworking, chemical, plastics, fertilizer, rubber tire, aerospace, motorcycle, elevator, electrical and electronic engineering, food processing, watch and clock, building materials, printing and publishing, and consumer goods industries. It is a route hub and has an international airport and a subway system.

Much of the city was wrecked in World War II, but many historic buildings remain or were reconstructed. Along Andriyivskky Descent are an early-twentieth-century mock "castle," the baroque church of Saint Andrew, and other historic buildings. The Kiev Pechersk Lavra (the Monastery of the Caves), dating from the eleventh century, includes medieval and later cathedrals, as well as bell towers, monuments, and underground cave systems; some of its churches are reconstructions. The downtown area is centered around wide Independence Square and Khreschatyk Street. The city has theaters, concert halls, museums and art galleries, a zoo, many parks, gardens (including two botanical gardens), and open spaces, especially along the western bank of the Dnieper, which contains a number of islands.

C. CARPENTER

A view of Kiev along the wide Dnieper River.

Dnipropetrovs'k

Dnipropetrovs'k is the major industrial base in central Ukraine. The city lies along the Dnieper River.

In 2007, the Dnipropetrovs'k (formerly Dnepropetrovsk) metropolitan area had a population of 1,480,000 people, while 1,056,000 people lived within the city limits. The metropolitan area includes Dniprodzerzhysk (formerly Dneprodzerzhinsk), which had a population of 250,000 in the same year.

THE DEVELOPMENT OF DNIPROPETROVS'K

At some time in the ninth century CE, Byzantine Orthodox monks founded a monastery on an island in the Dnieper River where Dnipropetrovs'k now stands, but it was destroyed by a Tatar invasion in 1240. For several centuries, there was little settlement in the region, which became a border district of Poland-Lithuania, whose eastern frontier in the region was formed by the Dnieper. The Poles founded a fort nearby in 1635, but the Russian settlement of Ekaterinoslav was not established along the north bank of the Dnieper until 1783. Three years later, the township was reestablished along the south bank. From 1792 through 1802, the town was renamed Novorosiysk, but the name Ekaterinoslav was restored in 1802.

During the nineteenth century, Ekaterinoslav's position began to be important. The Dnieper River offered navigation inland and to the Black Sea. The city was a bridging point of the Dnieper and, when railroads were constructed in the 1880s, connections with Moscow to the north, the Donbas coalfield to the east, and the port of Odesa were established. Industrialization followed, and the city rapidly developed. From a population of 12,000 in 1840, Ekaterinoslav grew to be home to 39,000 by 1880, 121,000 by 1900, and 169,000 in 1920. After the Russian Revolution (1917) and the establishment of the Soviet Union (1922), the Soviet authorities greatly developed the industries of the city and, in 1926, renamed it Dnepropetrovsk. Through the 1920s and 1930s, the industrialization of the city increased; in 1939, Dnepropetrovsk was home to some 537,000 people. The city was occupied by the Germans from 1941 through 1944, during World War II (1939–1945). In the late 1960s through early 1980s, the city flourished, in part because of the influence of what came to be known as the Dnepropetrovsk Faction, a group of powerful figures in the Soviet Communist Party, including Leonid Brezhnev (1906–1982; in office as general secretary of the Communist Party of the Soviet Union and effectively ruler of the Soviet Union 1964–1982), who came from the area.

THE MODERN CITY

Powerful patrons and the city's location helped Dnepropetrovsk develop as one of the major Soviet industrial bases in the second half of the twentieth century. It became one of the most important centers of the Soviet space, nuclear, and arms industries. The city's industries were powered by coal from the Donbas and by electricity from a string of huge hydroelectric power facilities constructed along the Dnieper River. Dnepropetrovsk has a large iron and steel industry, as well as facilities making metal plates and sheets, castings and tubes, railroad rails and locomotives, mining and other heavy engineering equipment. Other industries include tires, chemicals and plastics (based on coal), food processing, paint, clothing and shoes, radio equipment, and a range of consumer goods industries. The clothing industry prepares items for western European and Canadian corporations, and the aerospace industry is still a major sector, despite the demise of the Soviet Union.

A wide boulevard traverses the downtown; this street and October Square are lined by the main public buildings, including the eighteenth-century cathedral. However, few other historic buildings remain; many churches were destroyed during the Soviet purges of the 1930s, and damage during World War II completed the destruction. The city has theaters, museums, concert halls, a subway, and an international airport. In modern times, the city, which has adopted the Ukrainian version of its name, Dnipropetrovs'k, has relatively few high-rise buildings. The city is relatively spacious, with parks and riverside areas. New office buildings tend to be constructed in older styles rather than multistory construction.

C. CARPENTER

A night view of Dnipropetrovs'k's modern buildings, which line the shore of the Dnieper River.

Kharkiv

Kharkiv (formerly given by its Russian name, Kharkov) had a population in the metropolitan area of 1,840,000 in 2007. In the same year, 1,465,000 people lived within the city limits.

Kharkiv occupies a strategic position at the convergence of three waterways, in northeastern Ukraine, close to the border with Russia. More than 45 percent of the city's inhabitants are ethnic Russians, and Kharkiv is predominantly Russian-speaking rather than Ukrainian-speaking. Kharkiv's population is declining, and, since the independence of Ukraine in 1991, the city's defense-based industries, which were important under the Soviet Union, have contracted.

THE DEVELOPMENT OF KHARKIV

There is evidence of settlement in the area now occupied by Kharkiv from the second millennium BCE, and it is known that people of the Chernyakhiv or Chernyakhov culture inhabited the site from the second through sixth centuries CE. However, a city was not founded until 1655, when Russia established a fortified settlement along what was then its southern frontier. Part of the walls of the fort, or kremlin, remain. The region's fertile soils promoted an agricultural economy, and the town's position, a natural route hub, helped its development. By 1732, Kharkov was a provincial capital. The arrival of the railroad in 1869, connecting Kharkov with the Donets coalfield, spurred industrialization. As a result, the city's population grew through the nineteenth century, from 10,000 in 1811, to 45,000 in 1858, 128,000 in 1890, 174,000 in 1897, and 206,000 by 1904.

After the establishment of the Ukrainian Soviet Socialist Republic (SSR) in 1917, Kharkov became the first state capital of the Communist republic, a role it fulfilled until 1934, when the

Examples of imperial architecture still lining the streets of Kharkiv include this building on Sumskaya Street.

government of the Ukrainian SSR moved to Kiev. The Soviet authorities developed industry in Kharkov, particularly heavy industry, engineering, and the arms industry and tank production. In the 1930s, famine drove many people from the countryside into the city. The Soviet authorities ordered the murder of some 3,800 Polish prisoners (army officers and others) in Kharkov in spring 1940; they were subsequently buried in Katyn Forest. In World War II (1939–1945), the city changed hands several times and, in four major battles for control of Kharkov between Soviet and German forces, much of the city was destroyed. As a result, the downtown area was subsequently reconstructed with broad avenues and monumental buildings in the Soviet style.

THE MODERN CITY

In modern times, the city's industries include engineering, such as machine tools, mining equipment, tractors, diesel locomotives, turbines and generators; food processing; consumer goods; and electrical and electronic industries. The city still makes tanks, which are exported to foreign armies. Since independence, the Ukrainian version of the city's name has been used. Kharkiv is a cultural, commercial, educational, and retail center, with theaters and famous orchestras, three major universities, other higher educational institutions, and museums and other cultural institutions, most of them housed in buildings reconstructed since World War II.

The most prominent modern construction is Freedom Square (Poshcha Svobody in Ukrainian). Said to be the third-largest city square in Europe, Freedom Square includes gardens, is lined by multistory buildings, and terminates in a broad semicircle. The square is used for public meetings and concerts, and the surrounding part of the city contains many trees and gardens. Few old buildings survived the war, but those remaining include a monumental bell tower commemorating the Russian victory over the French in 1812 and two cathedrals, one constructed in the seventeenth century, the other in the nineteenth century.

The city is a route hub, with main highways and railroads converging from Kiev, the Ukrainian national capital; the Black Sea ports; the coalfields and industrial regions of eastern Ukraine; and Moscow, the Russian national capital. Kharkiv has an international airport, the second largest in Ukraine, and a subway system.

C. CARPENTER

the region known as the Donbas or the Donets Basin, with its large deposits of coal, as well as iron ore and manganese. In the same region, heavy metallurgy produces cast iron, rolled steel, and steel pipes, which found a ready market early in the twenty-first century as world demand for steel and steel products rose from 2000 through 2008. Coal mining is still important, and the large chemical industry uses coal to manufacture many products.

Other industries produce mining equipment, metallurgical equipment, transportation equipment (railway locomotives, freight cars, seagoing vessels, trucks, and cars), and other types of heavy machinery (hydroelectric and thermal steam and gas turbines, electric generators, and hoisting and transportation equipment). Also, throughout the country, there are facilities producing equipment for agriculture and processing food, and many cities make textiles, clothing, and shoes. The Ukrainian food-processing industry includes producing vegetable oil and margarine from sunflower seeds, granulated sugar from sugar beets, and flour and baked goods from grain. Processing meat, fruit, and dairy products is also locally important. In coastal cities, such as Odesa, there are fish-processing companies. Wine making and distilling are also significant, especially in Transcarpathia and Crimea.

Ukraine inherited production facilities of the Soviet military-industrial system, and Kiev, Kharkiv, and other centers have scientific and technical facilities related to the defense industry. The nation is still an important exporter of arms and related products. However, some defense industry facilities now make commercial vehicles and tractors.

Odesa is a major port on the Black Sea.

sugar, and dairy products increased, boosting Ukrainian exports. The nation's main exports are steel and steel products and other metals, fuel and petroleum products, chemicals, machinery and transportation equipment, and food (particularly sugar). The main imports are petroleum and natural gas, machinery and equipment, and chemicals. Russia is the main trading partner; in 2007, Russia supplied 25 percent of Ukraine's imports and took 21 percent of Ukraine's exports. The other main suppliers of imports are Germany, China, Poland, and Turkmenistan, while Turkey, Italy, and United States are among major recipients of Ukrainian exports. Trade with European Union (EU) states is increasing.

SERVICES

Banking, retail trade, transportation, tourism, and communications are the fastest growing sectors of the economy. Until the fall of 2008, bank lending expanded, with the largest amount of investment going to retail, car services, household goods, and personal supplies. The award of the 2012 European (soccer) Championship finals jointly to Ukraine and Poland—to be staged at several cities in both countries—has boosted service industries, particularly hotel and catering. Tourism is still mainly internal, although Russian visitors come to beach resorts along the Crimean coast. Other tourist centers include Kiev, Odesa, the Carpathian Mountains, and Lviv.

TRADE

In 2007, Ukraine exported goods and services worth $49.8 billion but imported goods and services valued at $60.4 billion. As a result, the nation had a large trade deficit. However, in the early twenty-first century, demand for Ukrainian steel and metals, grain,

TRANSPORTATION AND COMMUNICATION

Ukraine has a highway network of 105,274 miles (169,422 km), of which 102,906 miles (165,611 km) are paved. The main highway system, connecting the main cities, is of a good standard and is heavily used for passenger and goods transportation. The nation has a railroad system of 13,964 miles (22,473 km), and Kiev, Kharkiv, Kryvyj Rih, and Dnipropetrovs'k have subway systems. Ukraine has ten international airports, of which Kiev is the largest. The main port is Odesa, and Kerch, Kherson, Mariupol, and Mykolayiv are also major ports. Navigation along the nation's waterways, particularly the Dnieper River, is still significant.

The communications system inherited at independence was out of date and inefficient, with more than 3 million potential customers awaiting connection. There has been much improvement, and most cities have digital networks. In 2007, there were nearly 12.9 million main telephone lines, and there were 55.5 million mobile cellular phones, which is considerably more than the nation's population. In the same year, some 10 million people had Internet access.

R.V. KASHBRASIEV

Further Research

WORLD GEOGRAPHY

Agnew, John, Katharyne Mitchell, and Gerard Toal, eds. *A Companion to Political Geography*. Hoboken, NJ: Wiley-Blackwell, 2007.

Aguado, Edward, and James E. Burt. *Understanding Weather and Climate*. Upper Saddle River, NJ: Prentice Hall, 2009.

Clark, Audrey, ed. *Longman Dictionary of Geography: Human and Physical*. New York: Longman, 1985.

Duncan, James, Nuala Johnson, and Richard Schein. *A Companion to Cultural Geography*. Hoboken, NJ: Wiley-Blackwell, 2007.

Lomolino, Mark V., Brett R. Riddle, and James H. Brown. *Biogeography*. Sunderland, MA: Sinauer Associates, 2005.

Lutgens, Frederick K., Edward J. Tarbuck, and Dennis Tasa. *Essentials of Geology.* Upper Saddle River, NJ: Prentice Hall, 2008.

McKnight, Tom L., and Darrel Hess. *Physical Geography: A Landscape Appreciation*. Upper Saddle River, NJ: Prentice Hall, 2007.

National Geographic Family Reference Atlas. Washington, DC: National Geographic Society, 2006.

Strahler, Alan H., and Arthur Strahler. *Modern Physical Geography*. Hoboken, NJ: John Wiley and Sons, 1992.

Times Comprehensive Atlas of the World. London: HarperCollins Publishers, 2008.

REGIONAL GEOGRAPHY, HISTORY, AND CULTURAL EXPRESSION

Arnold, E. Nicholas. *Reptiles and Amphibians of Europe*. Princeton, NJ: Princeton University Press, 2003.

Blanning, T. C. W. *The Oxford Illustrated History of Modern Europe*. New York: Oxford University Press, 2001.

Blanning, T. C. W. *The Nineteenth Century: Europe, 1789–1914*. New York: Oxford University Press, 2000.

Blouet, Brian W. *The EU and Neighbors: A Geography of Europe in the Modern World*. Hoboken, NJ: John Wiley and Sons, 2007.

Bonney, Richard. *The European Dynastic States, 1494–1660*. New York: Oxford University Press, 1992.

Coldstream, Nicola. *Medieval Architecture*. New York: Oxford University Press, 2002.

Craske, Matthew. *Art in Europe, 1700–1830*. New York: Oxford University Press, 1997.

Crompton, Rosemary, Suzan Lewis, and Clare Lyonette. *Women, Men, Work, and Family in Europe*. New York: Palgrave Macmillan, 2007.

Cunliffe, Barry. *Europe between the Oceans: 9000 BC–AD 1000*. New Haven, CT: Yale University Press, 2008.

Cunliffe, Barry. *The Oxford Illustrated History of Prehistoric Europe*. New York: Oxford University Press, 2001.

Favell, Adrian. *Eurostars and Eurocities: Free Movement and Mobility in Integrating Europe*. Hoboken, NJ: Wiley-Blackwell, 2008.

Gilbert, Jean. *European Festivals: Songs, Dances, and Customs from around Europe*. New York: Oxford University Press, 2000.

Goldstein, Darra, and Kathrin Merkle. *Culinary Cultures of Europe: Identity, Diversity, and Dialogue*. Strasbourg: Council of Europe Publications, 2005.

Heffernan, Michael. *The Meaning of Europe: Geography and Geopolitics*. London: Hodder Arnold, 1998.

Hollister, C. Warren, and Judith Bennett. *Medieval Europe: A Short History*. Columbus, OH: McGraw-Hill, 2005.

Judt, Tony. *Postwar: A History of Europe since 1945*. New York: Penguin Books, 2006.

Kidner, Frank L., Maria Bucur, Ralph Mathisen, and Sally McKee. *Making Europe: People, Politics, and Culture*. Florence, KY: Wadsworth Publishing, 2007.

Macdonald, David W. *Mammals of Europe*. Princeton, NJ: Princeton University Press, 2001.

Merriman, John. *A History of Modern Europe: From the Renaissance to the Present*. New York: W. W. Norton, 2004.

Mullarney, Killian, Lars Svensson, Dan Zetterstrom, and Peter J. Grant. *Birds of Europe*. Princeton, NJ: Princeton University Press, 2000.

Parker, David. *Revolutions: The Revolutionary Tradition in the West, 1560–1991*. New York: Routledge, 2000.

Pinder, David, ed. *The New Europe: Economy, Society, and Environment*. Hoboken, NJ: Wiley, 1998.

Pounds, Norman J. G. *An Historical Geography of Europe, 1500–1840*. New York: Cambridge University Press, 2009.

Rapport, Michael. *Nineteenth Century Europe*. New York: Palgrave Macmillan, 2005.

Roberts, J. M. *Europe, 1880–1945 (General History of Europe)*. Harlow: Longman Publishing Group, 2001.

Tutin, T. G., V. H. Heywood, N. A. Burges, and D. H. Valentine. *Flora Europaea*. New York: Cambridge University Press, 2001.

Unwin, Tim, ed. *A European Geography*. Upper Saddle River, NJ: Prentice Hall, 1998.

Wilkinson, James D. *Contemporary Europe: A History.* Upper Saddle River, NJ: Prentice Hall, 2003.

TRAVEL LITERATURE

Elliott, Mark. *Russia and Belarus*. London: Lonely Planet, 2006.

Fodor's. *Moscow and St. Petersburg*. New York: Fodor's, 2006.

Hodges, Linda, and George Chumak. *Language and Travel Guide to the Ukraine*. New York: Hippocrene Books, 2009.

Insight Guides, eds. *Russia, Belarus, and Ukraine*. Duncan, SC: Insight Guides, 2009.

Johnstone, Sarah. *Ukraine*. London: Lonely Planet, 2005.

Roberts, Nigel. *Belarus*. Chalfont St. Peter, UK: Bradt Travel Guides, 2008.

BELARUS, RUSSIA, UKRAINE: HISTORY

Fritz, Verena. *State-Building: A Comparative Study of Ukraine, Lithuania, Belarus, and Russia*. New York: Central European University Press, 2008.

King, Charles. *The Ghost of Freedom: A History of the Caucasus*. New York: Oxford University Press, 2008.

Longworth, Philip. *Russia: The Once and Future Empire from Pre-History to Putin*. New York: St. Martin's Press, 2006.

Magocsi, Paul Robert. *A History of Ukraine*. Toronto: University of Toronto Press, 1996.

Montefiore, Simon Sebag. *Stalin: The Court of the Red Tsar*. London: Vintage, 2005.

Parker, Stewart. *The Last Soviet Republic: Alexander Lukashenko's Belarus*. Victoria, BC: Trafford Publishing, 2007.

Riasanovsky, Nicholas V., and Mark Steinberg. *A History of Russia*. New York: Oxford University Press, 2004.

Service, Robert. *A History of Modern Russia: From Nicholas II to Vladimir Putin*. Cambridge, MA: Harvard University Press, 2005.

Yekelchyk, Serhy. *Ukraine: Birth of a Modern Nation*. New York: Oxford University Press, 2007.

RUSSIA: GENERAL AND CULTURE

Bazán, Emilia Pardo. *Russia: Its People and Its Literature*. Boston, MA: Adamant Media Corporation, 2001.

Bucher, Greta. *Daily Life in Imperial Russia*. Westport, CT: Greenwood Press, 2008.

Cracraft, James, ed. *Architectures of Russian Identity, 1500 to the Present*. Ithaca, NY: Cornell University Press, 2003.

Figes, Orlando. *Natasha's Dance: A Cultural History of Russia*. New York: Picador, 2003.

Freeborn, Richard. *Dostoevsky (Life and Times)*. London: Haus Publishers, 2005.

Heretz, Leonid. *Russia on the Eve of Modernity: Popular Religion and Traditional Culture under the Last Tsars*. New York: Cambridge University Press, 2008.

Ledeneva, Alena V. *How Russia Really Works: The Informal Practices That Shaped Post-Soviet Politics and Business*. Ithaca, NY: Cornell University Press, 2006.

Politkovskaya, Anna. *Putin's Russia: Life in a Failing Democracy*. New York: Holt Paperbacks, 2007.

Richmond, Yale. *From Nyet to Da: Understanding the New Russia*. Boston, MA: Intercultural Press, 2008.

Volkov, Solomon. *Magical Chorus: A History of Russian Culture from Tolstoy to Solzhenitsyn*. London: Vintage Books, 2009.

UKRAINE: GENERAL

Aslund, Anders. *How Ukraine Became a Market Economy and Democracy*. Washington, DC: Peterson Institute for International Economics, 2009.

Helbig, Oksana Buranbaeva, and Vanja Mladineo. *Culture and Customs of Ukraine*. Westport, CT: Greenwood Press, 2008.

Mittica, Pierpaolo. *Chernobyl: The Hidden Legacy*. New York: Trolley Press, 2007.

Wilson, Andrew. *Ukraine's Orange Revolution*. New Haven, CT: Yale University Press, 2006.

BELARUS: GENERAL

Ioffe, Grigory. *Understanding Belarus and How Western Foreign Policy Misses the Mark*. Lanham, MD: Rowman & Littlefield Publishers, 2008.

Legvold, Robert, and Sherman W. Garnett. *Belarus at the Crossroad*. Washington, DC: Carnegie Endowment for International Peace, 2000.

Parker, Stewart. *The Last Soviet Republic: Alexander Lukashenko's Belarus*. Victoria, BC: Trafford Publishing, 2007.

PERIODICALS AND OTHER MEDIA

Belarusian Digest.
http://www.belarus-misc.org/bel-dusa.htm#belreview
Journal of Ukrainian Studies.
http://www.utoronto.ca/cius/webfiles/jus.htm
The Russian Review.
http://www.russianreview.org
Ukrainian Journal.
http://www.ukrainianjournal.com

ELECTRONIC SOURCES

Euromonitor International (country, market, and lifestyle information)
http://www.euromonitor.com/Belarus
http://www.euromonitor.com/Russia
http://www.euromonitor.com/Ukraine
The World Factbook. CIA.
www.cia.gov/library/publications/the-world-factbook/index.html (for facts about Belarus, Russia, Ukraine).
Tourism and culture in Belarus.
http://www.eng.belarustourism.by
Tourism and culture in Russia.
http://www.russia-travel.com/
Tourism and culture in the Ukraine.
http://www.traveltoukraine.org/index.htm

Index

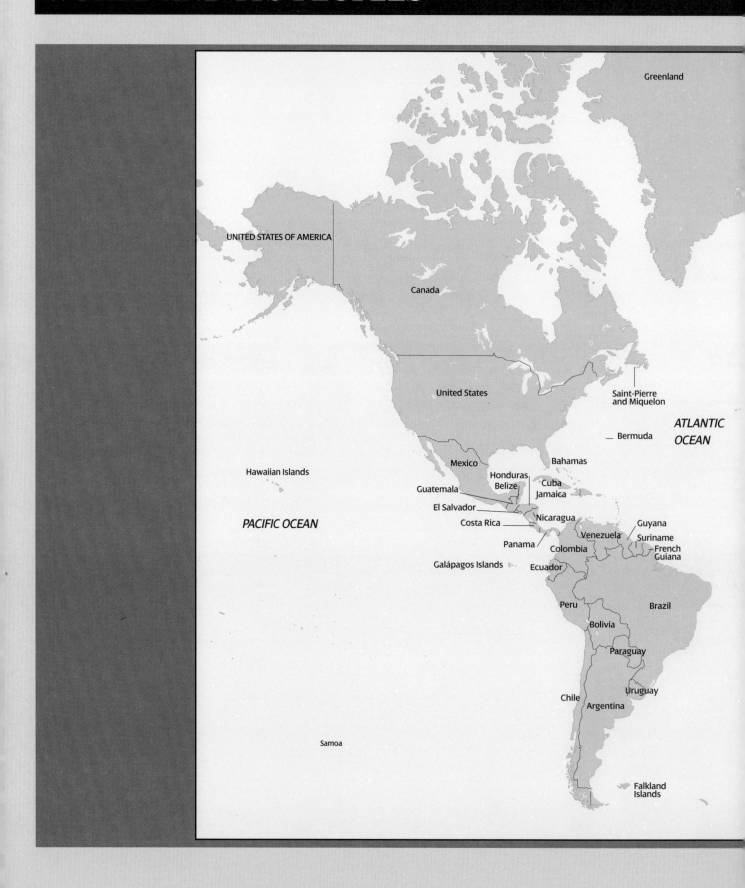

Greenland

UNITED STATES OF AMERICA

Canada

United States

Saint-Pierre
and Miquelon

ATLANTIC
OCEAN

Bermuda

Hawaiian Islands

Mexico

Bahamas

Honduras
Belize

Cuba
Jamaica

Guatemala

PACIFIC OCEAN

El Salvador

Nicaragua

Costa Rica

Guyana

Venezuela

Suriname

Panama

Colombia

French
Guiana

Galápagos Islands

Ecuador

Peru

Brazil

Bolivia

Paraguay

Uruguay

Chile

Argentina

Samoa

Falkland
Islands